MARGARET TUDOR

MARGARET TUDOR

TUDOR

THE LIFE OF HENRY VIII'S SISTER

MELANIE CLEGG

PEN & SWORD **HISTORY**

AN IMPRINT OF PEN & SWORD BOOKS LTD
YORKSHIRE – PHILADELPHIA

First published in Great Britain in 2018 by
PEN AND SWORD HISTORY
an imprint of
Pen and Sword Books Ltd
47 Church Street
Barnsley
South Yorkshire S70 2AS

ISBN 978 1 47389 315 3

Printed and bound in the UK by TJ International, Padstow, Cornwall.

Typeset in Times New Roman 11/13.5 by
Aura Technology and Software Services, India

Pen & Sword Books Ltd incorporates the imprints of Pen & Sword
Archaeology, Atlas, Aviation, Battleground, Discovery,
Family History, History, Maritime, Military, Naval, Politics, Railways,
Select, Social History, Transport, True Crime, Claymore Press,
Frontline Books, Leo Cooper, Praetorian Press, Remember When,
Seaforth Publishing and Wharncliffe.

For a complete list of Pen and Sword titles please contact
Pen and Sword Books Limited
47 Church Street, Barnsley, South Yorkshire, S70 2AS, England
E-mail: enquiries@pen-and-sword.co.uk
Website: www.pen-and-sword.co.uk

Contents

Acknowledgements

I first became interested in the life of Margaret Tudor while I was writing about her daughter-in-law Marie de Guise, and eventually decided that it made sense to focus specifically on her at some point in the future. Although she deserves her place in history books thanks to the important role that she played in sixteenth-century royal politics and also, more specifically, the drama surrounding the Tudor succession after Henry VIII, Margaret has rarely had the attention that the rest of her family have enjoyed and when she has merited a mention, has received a pretty hard time from historians thanks to her poor decision-making and the chaos of her marital history. Having said that, the main reason I found Margaret so fascinating was the way that her story often mirrored that of her granddaughter Mary Queen of Scots, who could have learned a great deal from the misfortunes that befell her and yet never quite did.

As always this book is dedicated to my amazing friends, who have put up with months of complaining while I completed this book; my lovely boys, who took absolutely no interest whatsoever but might have paid a bit more attention if Margaret was a character in Assassin's Creed, and Simon Hayden, who is still persevering with the cups of tea, even if I never actually drink them. In fact, I have one cooling next to me at this very moment. Sorry Simon!

Above all though, I'd like to dedicate this book to Margaret herself. One of the things I noticed during my research was that there were no contemporary mentions of her having any friends, with I thought was really sad. Both Marie de Guise and Henrietta Anne, my last two subjects, were singularly blessed with their friendships and clearly had no problems at all inspiring affection and loyalty in those who came into close contact with them – even, on occasion, with people who really did not want to like them. They both had their problems, but were constantly buoyed up by the love and support of their close knit families and friends, whereas poor Margaret doesn't seem to have had anyone on her side. I kept finding myself shaking

ACKNOWLEDGEMENTS

my head and thinking: 'Good grief, this woman really needed some friends to stage an intervention or just take her out for a drink', when I was writing so I think it only right to dedicate the book to her with the very late-in-the-day offer to be her friend, get her drunk and delete Archibald Douglas's number from her phone and probably tell her brother Henry to get lost too.

Chapter 1

The Rise of the Tudors 1485–1489

Margaret Tudor's future fate, and that of all her siblings, was decided on a field near Leicester on 22 August 1485 when her father Henry Tudor, Earl of Richmond, defeated and killed the last Yorkist King Richard III and seized the crown of England for himself. Although Henry's claim to the throne was so negligible as to be virtually non-existent, the strength of his supporters and decisiveness of his victory meant that his extraordinary rise to supreme power was largely uncontested. Henry's coup was made all the more concrete when he announced his intention to take Richard's eldest niece Elizabeth of York as his wife, using her as the means to bring the last remaining Yorkist supporters to heel. This match, secretly brokered by the putative couple's respective mothers and which had seemed so desirable when the ambitious pretender Henry was canvassing for support before his invasion of England, was actually as problematic as everything else about his quest for power – Richard III's claim to the throne had been based on the *Titulus Regius*, an official edict which presented as indisputable fact the dubious tale that his brother, Elizabeth's father Edward IV had already been secretly married to another aristocratic beauty, Lady Eleanor Butler when he took her mother Elizabeth Woodville as his wife, which meant that the ten children that this fruitful royal marriage had produced were all in fact illegitimate and as such, had as little claim to the throne as Henry, the descendant of John of Gaunt's extra-marital liaison with Katherine Swynford, himself.

The issue was further complicated by the fact that Elizabeth's younger brothers, Edward V and Richard, Duke of York, had not been seen since 1483 and were presumed dead, possibly murdered by their uncle Richard as part of his own bid for power – although the boys could just as easily have died of natural causes in the fetid atmosphere of the Tower of London. Naturally it suited Henry very well if the boys were assumed to be long-dead, but persistent rumours that either one or both of them had survived would continue to dog his reign and cast doubts upon his own right to rule. It also suited him to temporarily leave the five surviving daughters of Edward IV and Elizabeth Woodville in limbo by refusing to immediately reverse the official edict that had rendered them all illegitimate and removed them from the succession. Although it must surely have occurred to a man as cunning and intelligent as Henry Tudor that it might be better for him to repudiate his betrothal with Elizabeth and instead pursue a more prestigious match with a French noblewoman, cementing his friendship with Charles VIII, he stood firm – her prestige may have been harmed by the controversy surrounding her parents' marriage but Elizabeth still had enormous value to Henry as the eldest surviving Yorkist heir, while her suitability to rule at his side was undisputed. Elizabeth, blessed with all the good health, intelligence and beauty of her famously charming and good looking parents, had been carefully reared since birth to one day wear a crown – at the age of 9 she had been betrothed to the Dauphin of France and, until the marriage was called off seven years later, had been encouraged to think of herself as the future Queen of France.

However, any Yorkist diehards who had expected Henry to immediately reestablish Elizabeth's legitimacy and status before claiming the throne on her behalf were doomed to disappointment. Although well aware of his own poor claim to the throne, Henry was nonetheless determined to make it clear from the start that all power devolved to him, and that he alone was the rightful monarch. While another man might have sought to reinforce such a weak claim by underlining the dynastic rights of his wife, Henry, who was no fool, decided that his best chance of retaining the crown that he had fought so long and hard for was to tough it out and refuse to neither apologise for or even acknowledge the weakness of his claim. It isn't known what Elizabeth thought of this, but in public at least she never behaved with anything other than meek acquiescence to her husband's will. She may have been brought up to be a queen one day, but she had also been carefully reared, like all noblewomen of her time, to cede all authority to her husband and this she proceeded to do, apparently totally content to be demoted to the rank of consort rather than joint ruler.

One of Henry's first actions after his victory at Bosworth was to send a message to Elizabeth, who was residing in Sheriff Hutton Castle in Yorkshire, requesting that she return to London and there await further instructions. However, if she was expecting him to immediately honour his side of the agreement and take her to be his wife then she was sorely disappointed, for although Henry punctiliously visited her and clearly admired her good looks and charm, he made no move to make her his wife. Although this hesitancy was mostly motivated by Henry's natural caution and desire to side-line Elizabeth's claim to the throne, it may also have had something to do with the stories he had heard about the close relationship which had existed between his prospective bride and her uncle, Richard III. Although no concrete evidence exists that Richard had been anything more than an affectionate uncle to his eldest brother's daughters, still unpleasant rumours persisted that not only had he been planning to marry his eldest niece Elizabeth, but that she had been actively encouraging his advances. Although we have no way of knowing what Henry made of these stories, he may well have felt piqued enough to want to punish Elizabeth a little by leaving her in a state of some uncertainty about her future – although *Titulus Regius* had been repealed shortly after his arrival in the capital, restoring the princess and her sisters to legitimacy.

However, it was not until 18 January 1486, almost six months after his triumph at Bosworth and two and a half months after his coronation as sole monarch that Henry took Elizabeth of York as his wife in a splendid ceremony at Westminster Abbey. She would have to wait almost two years for her own coronation, which took place in November 1487, fourteen months after the birth of her first child, Prince Arthur, whose arrival, albeit a month prematurely, almost exactly nine months after his parents' wedding, was regarded as a pleasing omen for the future strength and success of the fledgling Tudor dynasty, as well as a confirmation of the blessed fruitfulness of this new alliance between the former warring houses of York and Lancaster. Nonetheless, Elizabeth was not to conceive again until the spring of 1489 – possibly on the advice of her doctors, who may have advised caution after the premature arrival of Prince Arthur and her subsequent lengthy bout of ill health, during which she struggled to recover from her ordeal and was laid low by a mild fever. It's also possible that she suffered a series of miscarriages after the arrival of Prince Arthur, but if this was the case, these sad losses occurred at such an early stage that they warranted no official mention and were instead private tragedies, discreetly endured by the royal couple and their immediate circle.

Elizabeth and Henry were spending Easter at Windsor Castle when the royal physicians confirmed that the royal nursery, where 3-year-old Prince Arthur currently dwelled in a state of solitary splendour as befitted the heir to the throne, was about to welcome a new addition. The pregnancy passed without incident and on 31 October 1489, the heavily pregnant Elizabeth, attended by great ceremony, vanished into her bedroom at the Palace of

Westminster, which had been transformed into a dark and womblike birthing chamber for the hallowed event of the imminent royal birth.

> On All-Hallows Eve, the Queen took to her chamber at Westminster, royally accompanied with ladies and gentlemen, that is to say, with my lady the King's mother, the Duchess of Norfolk and many other going before her, and besides greater part of the nobles of the realm assembled at Westminster at the Parliament. She was led by the Earl of Oxford and the Earl of Derby. The reverend father in God, the Bishop of Exeter, said Mass in his pontificals in St Stephen's Chapel. The Earls of Shrewsbury and of Kent held the towels when the Queen received the Host, and the corners of the towels were golden, and the torches were holden by knights; and after Agnus Dei was sung, and the bishop ceased, the Queen was led as before. When she was come unto her great chamber, she tarried in the anteroom before it, and stood under her cloth of estate. Then was ordained a void (drink) of spices and sweet wines. That done, my lord the Queen's chamberlain, in very good words, desired in the Queen's name all her people there present to pray that God would send her a good hour.

Rich blue arras cloth decorated with multitudes of gold fleurs-de-lis covered the walls, windows and ceiling of the inner birthing chamber, while the room was furnished with every possible luxury and comfort that the royal coffers could provide. A lot of the rich baby items that had been purchased for the birth of Prince Arthur, such as his enormous, elaborate oak cradle with ermine, blue velvet and crimson cloth-of-gold trimmings and cloth-of-gold canopy, were doubtless reused for the event though. When Elizabeth was pregnant with Arthur, Henry and Margaret had worked together on updating the ordinances that dictated how royal ceremonials at his court should be run and which specified even the most trivial details, such as the colour, quality and quantity of sheets provided when the queen gave birth, what she should wear before, during and after the birth, and how her state bed should be made up by her gentlewomen. The birth itself took place not in the magnificent state bed, but a pallet bed placed at its foot, which was elaborately and comfortably furnished with 'a marvellous rich canopy of gold with a velvet pall garnished with bright red roses, embroidered with two rich panes of ermine covered with Rennes of lawn'. There, Elizabeth, dressed in a fresh nightgown and 'round mantle of crimson velvet, plain, furred with ermines', would give birth, surrounded by the ladies of her household and attended to by an experienced female midwife, Alice Massey, who was paid £10 for her services.

Childbirth at this time was an intensely female and even mysterious affair, during which women supported each other and the labouring mother, who was at significant risk of actually dying in the process, was encouraged to think not about earthly matters but rather contemplate her proximity to God himself – as evidenced by the altar that stood at the foot of the birthing bed so that she could gaze upon the cross during her own sufferings. Men, other than the baby's father and priests should events take an unfortunate turn, were usually banned from the hallowed precincts of the birthing chamber and would not be admitted until after the new mother, if she survived her ordeal, had been 'churched' and ritually cleansed of sin. The fact that childbirth might well end in tragedy was reflected in the ceremony that had preceded Elizabeth's entry into the birthing chamber, during which she had solemnly said her goodbyes not just to her husband and his nobility, but also the male members of her household, who might well never see her alive again. According to tradition, their roles were taken over by women for the duration. Although Elizabeth was young and healthy, there were some concerns about the outcome as she had suffered a great deal with her previous labour and had been laid low for quite some time afterwards. The midwives would have come prepared with herbal concoctions intended to make the labouring woman more comfortable even if, at this time, there was nothing that could entirely deaden her pain, while the cathedrals and abbeys of the realm would have been asked to donate holy relics that were considered especially beneficial for labouring women.

Like nowadays, it was considered important for women to have the support of their mothers and close female relatives while in labour and Elizabeth was no exception. Her mother Elizabeth Woodville, who had taken up residence at Bermondsey Abbey the day after her eldest daughter's twenty-first birthday in February 1487, returned to court for the event and remained with the young queen in the birthing chamber. Herself a veteran of twelve births, Elizabeth Woodville no doubt had plenty of helpful advice to offer on the topic – unlike her daughter's mother-in-law, Lady Margaret Beaufort, who had only given birth once and then in the most traumatic of circumstances as she was only 13-years-old at the time. Both Margaret and Elizabeth Woodville were present when Elizabeth privately received the new French Ambassador, François de

Luxembourg, along with three of his entourage and two male members of her household, in her apartments – the usual rule about men not being admitted to the queen's birthing chambers having been bent because he was one of her mother's cousins. It was no doubt a welcome respite from the endless tedium of what was to be almost exactly a month of seclusion before the baby, who turned out to be a princess rather than the second prince that had no doubt been hoped for, finally arrived at quarter past nine on the night of 28 November, the queen's labour pains having begun that morning while most of the household were in the cavernous splendour of Westminster Hall watching her son Arthur being created a Knight of the Bath as a precursor to being declared Prince of Wales and Earl of Chester the following day.

Two days later on the feast day of St Andrew, the patron saint of both Scotland and pregnant women, the newborn princess was ceremoniously collected from her mother's arms as she recuperated in the great state bed, the queen being unable to attend religious ceremonies until she had been 'churched', and then carried with great pomp by Anne Fiennes, Marchioness of Berkeley through Westminster Hall and on to Saint Stephen's Chapel, hung with cloth-of-gold and richly carpeted for the occasion, in the precincts of the Palace of Westminster. As befitted the eldest daughter of a king, the baby princess was accompanied by the Earls of Arundel and Shrewsbury and carried beneath a splendid canopy borne by four knights while her ermine-trimmed crimson velvet train was carried by her mother's aunt, Katherine Woodville, Duchess of Buckingham. At the head of the procession walked the baby's unmarried maternal aunt, 14-year-old Princess Anne of York, who carried the beautiful white lace trimmed chrisom dress that would be put on the infant after baptism and used as its shroud should it die soon after birth.

The baby was christened Margaret, in honour of her paternal grandmother, by John Alcock, Bishop of Ely, then plunged three times into the especially warmed-up holy water inside the exquisite silver font lent by Canterbury Cathedral for the occasion. At the same moment Henry Bourchier, Earl of Essex, lit a taper symbolising the light of Christ and the triumph of good over the evil of the original sin that the church decreed the baby had been born with, and held it for a moment in the baby's hand while the 120 gentlemen and knights present set fire to the torches they had held during the ceremony. After this, Princess Margaret was confirmed as a Christian at the altar by the Archbishop of York with the Marchioness of Berkeley, who had held her throughout, acting as sponsor.

The little princess' godparents were George Talbot, Earl of Shrewsbury; John Morton, Archbishop of Canterbury and Chancellor of England; her formidable grandmother and namesake Lady Margaret Beaufort and Elizabeth Talbot, Duchess of Norfolk, the elder sister of Lady Eleanor Talbot who had allegedly been married to Edward IV when he married Elizabeth Woodville. In another sad connection, the Duchess's only child, Anne de Mowbray, who was heiress to her father's vast estates and fortune, had been briefly married to Queen Elizabeth's youngest brother Richard, Duke of York, before dying at the age of just 8. The appointing of a godmother with so many connections, albeit pretty negative, to the York ruling house was a significant one and no doubt designed to underline the perfect accord that now existed between the two ruling houses – as if the little princess currently squalling in the arms of the Marchioness of Berkeley wasn't proof enough that the war that had torn the whole nation apart for decades was now well and truly in the past. The ceremony ended with the godparents enjoying the traditional warming drink of spiced wine before once again the great procession, this time torchlit as the gentlemen carried their flaming torches aloft, wended its way back through the palace to where Elizabeth was impatiently waiting to have her baby back in her arms again. At the head of the procession was carried the sumptuous gifts donated by the baby's godparents – most pleasingly of all, a silver-gilt chest full of gold from her grandmother, which was no doubt intended to form the basis of the princess's future dowry. Her elder brother was already unofficially betrothed to Catalina, daughter of Ferdinand of Aragon and Isabel of Castile, so who knew what plans her ambitious father would have for his new daughter as he sought to increase the Tudor family's prestige both at home and overseas.

Like all royal children at this time, Margaret was not breastfed by her own mother but immediately consigned to the care of a wet-nurse, Alice Davy, who would remain with her until she was fully weaned in 1491 at the age of 2. Also employed to take care of the new royal baby was Alice Biwimble, who transferred from Prince Arthur's household, and two cradle rockers, Anne Maryland and Margaret Troughton. Elizabeth Tyrell, Lady Darcy, who had cared for the children of Edward IV and Elizabeth Woodville now presided over the royal nurseries, although her duties mostly involved caring for the more important Prince Arthur, whose nursery court was based in Farnham in Hampshire. The new baby Margaret did not join him but was instead installed at the royal palace at Eltham on the outskirts of London, which was within easy reach of her parents' palace at Greenwich.

Eltham Palace had been a favourite residence of Margaret's grandfather Edward IV and he had done much to improve it during his reign, adding new service buildings and royal apartments, which included one of the first long galleries in the country, where the royal children could play during bad weather, and an immense great hall where they would receive visitors and dine in state. Built on a hill which afforded a wonderful view of London, and surrounded by dense hunting forests, Eltham was considered to be a highly suitable location for the royal nursery, where the king's children could benefit from healthy fresh air. This view was underlined within a month of Margaret's birth when the court was hit by a deadly measles epidemic which killed a number of her mother's ladies, making it all the more imperative that she and her elder brother should be as far away from London as possible.

Chapter 2

A Royal Childhood 1489–1497

Although Elizabeth of York was firmly ensconced at Henry VII's side as his lawful wife and Queen of England, everyone knew that the real power behind the throne was his formidable and extremely intelligent mother Lady Margaret Beaufort, Countess of Richmond and Derby. Having plotted and schemed for decades on behalf of her adored only son before he eventually seized the throne, Margaret was determined to enjoy every minute of her triumph while at the same time devoting her extraordinary intellectual abilities to the service of the Tudor dynasty. Although she seemed extremely fond of her daughter-in-law Elizabeth, and even deferred to her when the two women were together in public, still she made a point of dressing equally finely and making it clear to court visitors that she expected equal deference at all times – and should be courted as assiduously as the actual queen. Although she had been separated from her son for much of his childhood, as one would expect from such an erudite woman, she had still taken a great interest in his upbringing and education and it seems that she took great pleasure in extending this interest to his children. Naturally, the eldest boy Prince Arthur was the focus of the lion's share of Lady Margaret Beaufort's attention but she had time for the others too, including the girls, although her own passion for learning does not appear to have inspired her to make great scholars of her granddaughters and their educational prowess in no way rivalled that of the next few generations of Tudor girls, particularly Elizabeth I and Lady Jane Grey.

The next arrival in the royal nursery at Eltham was Prince Henry, who was born in June 1491 when Margaret was about 18 months old and after him came another girl, Princess Elizabeth, in July 1492. Although the three would have frequently spent time with their parents, grandmother and elder brother, who as Prince of Wales still lived separately in his own household, on the whole they were left alone and kept well away from the capital. At Eltham the royal children lived in some state – their father was well aware that many of his subjects believed that he had no real right to the throne and was therefore keen to underline his royal status as much as possible, as evidenced by the updated book of ordinances and the high level of flamboyant display at his court.

Every state occasion was seen as yet another opportunity to fly the flag for the Tudor dynasty and increase their prestige and it was important to Henry that his children should live like princes and princesses. Later, far more established royal dynasties like the Windsors and Romanovs would feel secure and comfortable enough to enforce stark furnishings, plain clothes, simple food, camp beds and cold morning baths on their offspring – not so, Henry VII. His children had the best of everything and in return were expected to look and behave like miniature adults. The household accounts for the royal nursery are full of entries detailing the lavish clothes ordered for the Tudor children – gowns of velvet, damask and silk, trimmed with fur and worn over linen smocks, which would be changed multiple times a day in warm weather. Like modern parents, Henry and Elizabeth seem to have been particularly keen on dressing the princesses in matching or complimentary dresses – in April 1495, a tawny velvet gown trimmed with black tinsel (a shiny material) was ordered for Margaret while a black velvet gown trimmed with tawny tinsel was procured for her younger sister Mary and a few years later in August 1498 both girls would be bought matching gowns of green velvet trimmed with purple.

Very little is known about the daily routine of Henry VII's younger children, who had rather less care expended on their education than their brother Arthur, who was receiving thorough training for his future role as King of England and to that end had moved to Ludlow Castle in Herefordshire at the start of 1493. It is likely that their daily routine followed much the same pattern as that imposed upon their mother Queen Elizabeth when she was a child and which revolved around the daily timetable of religious devotion – it being considered of paramount importance that the king's offspring should grow up to be good Christians. The royal children, who each had their own self contained two room apartment comprising an inner bedchamber and outer reception room, would have been woken by their nurses at around six in order to be ready to attend Matins before they went down to the chapel to hear the morning Mass. They then enjoyed a simple breakfast of bread, eggs and meat washed down with ale before proceeding to their first lessons. Dinner was the main meal of the day but unlike now was served at around eleven in the morning. Fussiness was not tolerated and the children would have been expected to have perfect table manners and sample a little of everything that was offered to them at the table, eating with their fingers and wiping their hands on linen napkins that were draped over the shoulder for this purpose. Dinner was usually a very formal affair with multiple dishes and courses and to while away the time, the children may well have been read to as they ate, with suitably inspiring or uplifting books being chosen for this purpose. Even when they were very young, mealtimes were seen as yet another opportunity to emphasise the rank and grandeur of the Tudor dynasty and so they were served by a full compliment of servants and with a great deal of ceremony beneath state cloths in the imposing great hall.

More lessons followed dinner, after which the Evensong bell would ring and they would all troop off to the chapel again before having a light supper of bread, meat and cheese at around four in the afternoon. The rest of the evening was devoted to leisure activities such as needlework, reading, playing games, dancing or music before the children had another light snack, charmingly called the 'all night', and went off to bed, usually at around eight, although they may well have stayed up later in the summer when the nights were lighter. It was a strictly governed routine, designed to fill every moment of their day while at the same time prepare them for the rigours of their future public lives, which might well involve presiding over their own courts. Idleness was considered to be gateway to sin and so the young Tudor princesses were never for a moment left to their own devices, but rather provided with a constant round of activities such as needlework, which could be picked up whenever they had any spare time to fill. Although they undoubtedly had some toys, such as the usual dolls – in Margaret's case as elaborately painted and dressed as any court lady – and carved wooden figures, right from the start their activities were all designed to prepare them for a useful and productive adulthood.

The Tudor royal children began their actual lessons early, first learning the simple prayers and psalms in their psalters before moving on to other subjects. Although the daughters of Henry VII did not benefit from the same vigorous education as their nieces and granddaughters, they were still considered extremely well educated at a time when the vast majority of women could not read or write anything other than perhaps their own name. With the literacy level of the general population so low, the little princesses, who were taught to read and write before the age of 5, probably seemed like paragons of learning, even though we know that Margaret was actually anything but. Although tutors were employed for all the royal children, it's very likely that Elizabeth herself taught her daughters to read and write, just as her own mother had taken the time to teach her – it being considered entirely appropriate for children to learn their first letters from their mothers. Otherwise, while their brothers were being taught Latin, French, philosophy, mathematics, geometry and history, the girls skimmed over these subjects, learning just enough to prevent them from being entirely ignorant, and instead focused their attention on what was considered the more womanly art of running a household.

We may scoff nowadays, but these lessons in household administration were not about preparing girls for a life of domestic drudgery but rather equipping them with the skills that they would require in order to be able to run huge households and, if their husbands were absent for whatever reason, take charge of often vast estates, possibly even countries. It can't have hurt that they would also have learned some valuable mathematics and money management skills along the way. The rest of their time was employed learning how to play musical instruments, dance, sing and generally make themselves agreeable – and they would no doubt have often been advised to look to their graceful, always perfectly behaved mother for an example of how a great lady should conduct herself in both public and private.

Music was extremely important at the Tudor court and the royal children were encouraged to learn to play their own instruments, this being regarded as an essential skill at a time when people were expected to make their own entertainment. Although their brother Henry was the most talented musician in the family – becoming proficient in several instruments before he was out of his teens – his sisters were perhaps not quite so broadly skilled but both Margaret and Mary became excellent lutists and could also both play the clavichord, a type of stringed keyboard instrument similar to a harpsichord. Music was everywhere at court though from the boy chorists of the royal chapel to the lutists who played during dinner, while virtually every lady and most of the gentlemen there knew how to play at least one instrument and would be expected to do so for the entertainment of the gathered company. Skilled dancers were also much in demand at court, where the dancing was generally vigorous and could go on for most of the night on special occasions. At a time when young women, even the ones residing in the relatively lax atmosphere of court, were closely watched and forbidden to spend time alone with unrelated men, dancing was a convenient and socially acceptable way for members of the opposite sex to talk without being overheard, hold hands and get to know one another. The daughters of Henry VII and Elizabeth of York were expected to become accomplished dancers and indeed Margaret and Mary would both become skilful at the art – their favourite partner being their brother Henry who was an exceptionally energetic dancer. This love of vigorous exercise, is evident in their passion for the outdoor sports as well. All of the Tudors adored riding and hunting and would go out in all weathers in their extensive hunting grounds. Riding was a crucial skill at court, where one might be expected to spend long hours in the saddle either while hunting or on progress across the country, and the royal children had riding lessons from an early age. Margaret would also become extremely skilled at archery, another favourite Tudor sport.

Although the royal children spent most of their time with their own household at Eltham, they would be increasingly seen at court events, where King Henry was only too pleased to be able to show off his brood of charming, attractive offspring, who had all been blessed with the striking good looks, fair complexions and Plantagenet red-gold hair of their mother's family. The children would usually join their parents for Christmas, Easter and the other most significant festivals of the religious calendar and would be expected to be on their very best behaviour. Their grandmother Lady Margaret Beaufort was particularly quick to notice poor behaviour and any child, no matter how young, seen picking their nose, pulling faces, looking surly or yawning would be instantly whisked away back to the nursery. Usually though, ambassadors and visitors to court would comment favourably on the behaviour and appearance of the Tudor siblings, noting how well they danced and how well favoured and like their parents, both of whom were good looking, they all were. As soon as they were born, Henry had begun planning for their future marriages, and so it was of paramount importance to him that his children, whom he intended to use to further the prestige of the Tudor dynasty, should impress foreign visitors, particularly those from Scotland, Spain and France as they were the nations that he was most keen to ally himself with. While Margaret had probably always been intended for the Scottish King James IV, his second daughter Princess Elizabeth was intended for a match with François de Valois, Duc d'Angoulême, who was two years her junior and might well one day become heir to the French throne should his cousins Charles VIII and Louis d'Orléans (who would succeed Charles as Louis XII in 1498) die without male heirs.

One of the first glimpses that we get of Margaret at court is shortly before her fifth birthday at the end of October 1494, when she was present at the lavish celebrations for her younger brother Henry's ennoblement as Duke of York. This sumptuous, expensive ceremony and the ensuing festivities, which lasted for over a fortnight, were intended not just to ennoble the king's second son but also as a sharp riposte to the supporters of Perkin Warbeck, the latest pretender to the throne, who was claiming to be the hitherto missing Richard, Duke of York, second son of Edward IV and brother of Queen Elizabeth. Unlike the previous pretender, the rather pathetic Lambert Simnel, Walbeck had managed to amass significant support on the continent, largely from Henry VII's enemies, who saw him as a useful way of striking a blow against the Tudor dynasty. His chief supporter was Edward IV's sister Margaret of York, dowager Duchess of Burgundy, who almost certainly did not believe that he was her nephew but instead chose to exploit him as a means of needling King Henry, whom she absolutely loathed. The effect of her actions on her eldest niece Queen Elizabeth does not appear to have crossed her mind. Believing that a Burgundian funded invasion attempt was imminent, Henry decided that it would be politic to have his own second son, who was just 3-years-old, declared Duke of York as soon as possible, thus making it clear that the previous incumbent of the title was dead. Despite his later reputation for miserliness, Henry at this stage was not at all adverse to spending lavishly on public celebrations and the investiture of Prince Henry was no exception. A series of magnificent jousts took place at the Palace of Westminster, which Henry and Elizabeth watched from beneath two cloths of state on a stage covered in blue cloth spangled with hundreds of gold fleurs-de-lis. Beside them sat their eldest daughter Princess Margaret, who was described as 'the fairest young princess' in a new velvet gown. On 11 November, that day's joust was held in Margaret's honour, which was probably her first taste of taking the central role at a court celebration since her baptism, and she duly handed out the prizes, ruby and diamond rings, to the winners.

The following summer, Henry and Elizabeth set out on a progress that would take them across the Cotswolds and into the Midlands, where they visited their eldest son at Ludlow before travelling up to Lancashire, the traditional heartland of the Lancastrian cause. Their ultimate destination was Latham House, the great estate that belonged to Henry's father-in-law Thomas Stanley, Earl of Derby, where Lady Margaret Beaufort was waiting to act as their hostess. It seemed increasingly likely that Perkin Warbeck was about to stage his invasion and in response, Henry had decided that it would be an excellent idea to make an appearance on Lancastrian soil in order to confirm that he still had the support of the people who had placed him on the throne in the first place, not least his father-in-law, whose loyalty could not always be counted upon. The fact that he had his beautiful and extremely charming wife at his side would have been considered hugely beneficial to his cause, but their three youngest children, who were far too young for such an arduous and lengthy trip, remained behind at Eltham, where they could enjoy all of their usual summer pastimes.

Disaster struck on 14 September 1495 when the 3-year-old Princess Elizabeth, who was said to be the most lovely of the two princesses, died suddenly either from an illness or as the result of an accident. The king and queen, who were on their way back from the north, were devastated. Unfortunately, it was by no means unusual for parents to lose their children in infancy at this time, but that did not mean that Tudor parents, so often portrayed as callous when it came to the mortality of their offspring, did not feel these losses very deeply and especially so when it was the first of their children to die. Princess Elizabeth was brought from Eltham in great state and buried with a great deal of expensive pomp and ceremony on the north side of the chapel of St Edmund the Confessor in Westminster Abbey. According to custom, her grieving parents were not at the ceremony but they spent £318, a great deal of money at the time, to ensure that their daughter had a funeral that befitted her status and ensured that she would be remembered by erecting a simple tomb of black marble surmounted with a gilt effigy and Latin epitaph, now both sadly lost, although the rest of the tomb and its inscription has survived.

This must have been an extremely sad time for the two children left behind at Eltham Palace. Margaret and Henry had been close to their sister and her sudden loss would have shocked and distressed them both terribly, especially if it had in fact been the result of an accident. Although they were not permitted to accompany her body on its dolorous last journey back to London or attend the funeral at Westminster Abbey, they would have been able to say their last farewells while it lay in state, covered in cloth-of-gold and surrounded by candles, for eleven days in the chapel at Eltham. For several months, both children wore mourning, which for Margaret would have involved black gowns and kirtles fashioned from satin, damask silk and worsted, trimmed with fur when the weather got colder and worn with black bonnets. Her brother Henry would have been an equally sombre sight, as would the rest of their household at Eltham until the mourning period was over and life could resume again. Queen Elizabeth was already five months pregnant with her next child when Elizabeth died and the arrival of the new baby in the Eltham Palace nursery in March 1496 no doubt did much to raise everyone's spirits. For Margaret this new arrival was particularly welcome for it was another sister, who had been christened Mary, probably in honour of their mother's younger sister Mary of York who had died at the age of 14 in 1482. Whether Margaret continued to be fond of Mary as she blossomed into loveliness so rare and astonishing that even Erasmus would say of her that 'nature has never formed anything more beautiful', remained to be seen.

On 21 September 1496, Perkin Warbeck and his new ally James IV of Scotland marched their troops over the River Tweed at Coldstream and invaded the north of England. However, they got no further than four miles into Northumberland before word reached them that an English army was on its way to intercept them, at which point they turned around and returned to the safety of Scotland. Like Margaret, Dowager Duchess of Burgundy, James was almost certainly exploiting Warbeck for his own gain, which involved using him as leverage in negotiations with the Spanish and English, while at the same time being an annoying thorn in King Henry's side as he tried to finalise the details for his eldest son's marriage to the Spanish Infanta whose parents were naturally refusing to send their precious daughter to England while Warbeck remained at large. Whatever his true feelings may have been about Warbeck's claims, he nonetheless chose to display his confidence in him by arranging for the pretender to marry a Scottish noblewoman, Lady Catherine Gordon, who, luckily for her husband, was as beautiful as she was well connected. Henry was furious with both James and his protegé and called for Parliament to increase taxes in order to fund a war against Scotland, which they willingly did in early 1497.

This turned out to be a bad move on Henry's part though, for it proved to be the last straw for his already disgruntled and impoverished Cornish subjects who got together at the end of May and formed a plan to march on London. As soon as news of this latest grass roots rebellion arrived at Sheen Palace, Henry furnished Elizabeth with an armed escort and packed her off to Eltham to collect their children and take them to a place of safety while he rode south west with his troops to meet the rebels before they reached the capital. Having decided that the countryside was too unsafe, Elizabeth took 7-year-old Margaret and her two younger siblings to Coldharbour, her mother-in-law's comfortable riverside mansion on Upper Thames Street in the heart of the old City of London. They remained there for six days before the news from outside the capital grew so alarming that they hastily moved into the safety of the Tower of London, which must have been immensely thrilling for Margaret and her brother Henry but rather less so for their mother, who had already endured more than enough of that sort of thing and had probably hoped that her days of seeking sanctuary were well and truly over.

Meanwhile, the Cornish rebels, whose numbers had swelled to almost 20,000 as they marched across the country, had camped just outside London at Blackheath and were preparing to attack the City and seize the Tower of London. Unfortunately for Elizabeth and her children, the rebels were under the impression that her husband was in the Tower with them and unaware that he was in fact not too far away in Lambeth, waiting to intercept them with his own far superior army. Trapped inside the Tower while outside ordinary Londoners were in a state of panic as they prepared for the worst, Elizabeth could only pray that her husband would manage to rout the rebels before they made it into the capital. We can only imagine how greatly relieved she was when news arrived on 17 June, five days after she had entered the Tower with her children, that her husband had defeated the rebels at Blackheath and was on his way back to liberate her. The bells of every church in London were ringing as the royal family finally left the Tower of London and it no doubt made a great impression on both Margaret and Henry to see their father proclaimed as a hero and to make their way through streets packed with cheering crowds. Unlike their somewhat retiring mother and eldest brother, the two middle Tudor siblings adored being the centre of attention and to them public adulation was more intoxicating and exciting than any drug and just as addictive.

There were more celebrations four months later when news arrived that Perkin Warbeck had been captured at Beaulieu Abbey in Hampshire after yet another abortive attempt to wage war within England. He and James of Scotland had hoped to capitalise on the unrest in Cornwall by trying to kickstart a second rebellion there but a series of misadventures, mostly caused by Warbeck's own poor decision making, had resulted in him abandoning his army while they were advancing into Somerset and fleeing east, which brought him uncomfortably close to London. James of Scotland now washed his hands of Warbeck, who had become both a liability and an embarrassment, and began to sue for peace with the English. This pleasing turn of events, which naturally provoked much celebration at court, was to have direct consequences for Margaret, who became a significant factor in the ensuing negotiations between her father and the Scots.

Chapter 3

The Scottish Alliance 1496–1498

In the summer of 1496, the Spanish monarchs Ferdinand of Aragon and Isabel of Castile advised their Ambassador to London, Roderigo de Puebla, that they were deliberately keeping the King of Scotland sweet by allowing him to think they were considering his proposal to marry their middle daughter, the Infanta Maria. However, this was all a ruse as they had no intention of sanctioning the match and were hoping to marry Maria off to the heir to the French throne, Louis, Duc d'Orléans, should he manage to have his childless existing marriage to Jeanne de France dissolved by the Pope. Naturally it had occurred to everyone that the always less-than-friendly relations between Scotland and England would almost certainly be improved if their respective queens happened to be sisters, but as this happy solution was not on the table, their most Catholic Majesties of Spain privately suggested to their ambassador that perhaps King Henry might consider trying to marry one of his daughters to the Scottish king instead. At this time, Margaret, the eldest of Henry's daughters was not quite 7-years-old – very young, but the age where a girl of her rank might expect to hear talk about her future matrimonial prospects. It seems likely that Henry had always earmarked James for Margaret – the fact that he had leapfrogged over her to match her younger sister Elizabeth with François d'Angoulême certainly suggests that Margaret was already spoken for, in her father's mind at least, and it would make sense for him to secure Scotland's friendship via the age-old means of marrying one of his daughters to its king.

The only potential issue was that of age. James of Scotland turned 23 on 17 March 1496 and already had quite a reputation for amorous adventures with the ladies of his court, whereas his prospective bride, Princess Margaret was sixteen years younger and would not be ready for marriage for perhaps another six or seven years, which was a long time to make James wait. Nonetheless, negotiations tentatively began as a part of the wider discussion about the fate of James's former protégé Perkin Warbeck, who was now a very well-treated prisoner at the English court. His wife, the beautiful

Lady Catherine Gordon, was also received at court and thanks to her well-bred manners quickly found favour with Queen Elizabeth, who appointed her as one of her ladies of waiting. The presence of the cultured, lovely Lady Catherine no doubt did much to promote Scottish interests at the English court, where many still believed the Scots to be a backward, rude and barbaric race. She would also have been able to assuage any fears that Henry and Elizabeth might have had about their prospective son-in-law, King James, as she knew him personally and would be able to tell them that his reputation as one of the most intelligent, cultured and learned princes in Europe was well deserved.

James IV had been King of Scotland since the age of 15, when his father James III had been killed by his own rebellious nobility in the Battle of Sauchieburn in June 1488. The rebels had planned from the first to place James, then Duke of Rothesay, on the throne and the boy had colluded with their plans – only to feel wracked with guilt about his involvement in his father's death much later on. The truth was that relations between James and his father were at best strained, and at worst absolutely dysfunctional. To the annoyance of James and his mother, Margaret of Denmark, the old king had openly favoured his second son, the Duke of Ross, who was also confusingly called James, and as a result had become fatally estranged from the rest of his family. Nonetheless, when James succeeded as king he treated his younger brother well, kept him at court and seemed to bear him no rancour, which must have seemed unusually lenient, if not rather foolhardy, for the times.

In this as in most things however, James seemed determined to do things his own way. He was unconventional, curious, charming, handsome and liberal. In many ways he anticipated the reign of his descendant Charles II, another charming, intellectually curious man whose many passions also included horseflesh, music, science and beautiful women. To the few foreign visitors who came to the Scottish court, James seemed endlessly full of surprises and they reported back that he loved embroidery and would sit for hours sewing with his latest mistress; that he was fascinated by the practice of medicine, especially dentistry, and would pay his courtiers to allow him to extract their troublesome teeth and, most admirable of all, he was genuinely gifted with languages and could speak not only English but also Scots, Gaelic, Latin, French, German, Spanish, Italian, Flemish and Danish, the last of which he had learnt from his mother. He was in every way the epitome of the perfect Renaissance prince – energetic, inquisitive, charismatic, good looking and erudite – perhaps his contemporaries thought him sadly wasted in Scotland, but James himself certainly never thought so. He loved his country with a passion that far eclipsed the more fleeting infatuations he had for the ladies that caught his wandering eye, and believed that it was his duty, and destiny, to make Scotland a major player on the international stage.

As a child, James had been betrothed to Princess Cecily of York, the pretty younger sister of Queen Elizabeth and, ironically, this match with England had proved to be one of the factors in his father's undoing due to its unpopularity with his Scottish aristocracy and subjects. Naturally, James was cautious about negotiating another potentially polarising English match but he took comfort from both his popularity with his own people and also the fact that his international prestige had never been higher thanks to his patronage of Perkin Warbeck. He would have preferred one of the daughters of Ferdinand and Isabel but as none were available, the English match seemed to be his best option and so the negotiations began in earnest, although they proved to be long-winded and would drag on for several more years to come.

The Spanish monarchs took a particular interest in the affair as their daughter Catalina was betrothed to Prince Arthur and was, in fact, already being styled Princess of Wales and encouraged to practice her French and get used to drinking wine and ale (the water in England was considered extremely unhealthy) in preparation for her arrival at the English court. Ferdinand and Isabel had been deeply disturbed by the activities of the pretender Perkin Warbeck and were not especially reassured by King Henry's remarkably benign way of dealing with the now captive Warbeck and his Scottish wife. They wanted their daughter to go to a secure and safe court and to eventually in the fullness of time become Queen of England – the rumours about the survival of Queen Elizabeth's brothers, the presence at court of the Warbecks and the constant threat that more pretenders might be poised to come out of the woodwork, naturally made them very concerned about her long term prospects if she married into a family that might well lose their throne at any moment. It seemed to them that the mischievous young James of Scotland delighted in provoking King Henry and never failed to miss an opportunity to tease his neighbouring monarch – which was easily ignored if it involved the usual, relatively harmless but nonetheless tiresome border raids to steal cattle but obviously had far more serious ramifications for the future security of their daughter if he decided to harbour Yorkist pretenders to the throne or even go to war on their behalf. It was therefore entirely understandable that they should now be encouraging Henry to make a friend of James by marrying one of his daughters to him.

Princess Margaret's thoughts about the negotiations are unknown, although her later personality would suggest that she was probably eager to become a queen and enjoy all the benefits of high station. We do know, however, that her mother Elizabeth and grandmother Lady Margaret Beaufort took a very close interest in the matter and were particularly concerned about the character and reputation of the prospective bridegroom. Rumours of King James's sexual philandering with his two rival mistresses, Janet Kennedy and Margaret Drummond, had reached the English court, no doubt flamed by the disgruntled Warbeck, and the two royal ladies were understandably worried about Margaret's prospects for happiness as the wife of such a man. If King Henry had other lovers behind his wife's back then he was remarkably discreet about the fact so Elizabeth had no personal experience of the situation – but her father, Edward IV, had been a noted womaniser, which had indirectly led to Richard III's seizure of the throne and the death of her two brothers, and so she had every reason to be wary of James's reputation. Her mother had borne her father's indiscretions with remarkable grace, as she would also no doubt have done herself, but it was not a situation that any woman would want for her own daughter and so she had her concerns. For the more pragmatic Lady Margaret Beaufort, the main concern was her granddaughter's tender age. She herself had been married off at just 12-years-old to Henry VI's half brother Edmund Tudor, who was exactly twice her age, and had given birth to her only child, the future King Henry, just over a year later. Although the stoic Margaret rarely spoke of it, the experience was clearly a traumatic one as evidenced by her determination that her eldest granddaughter should not suffer the same fate. According to the Spanish Ambassador, Don Pedro de Ayala, King Henry himself confided in him that,

> the Queen and my mother are very much against the marriage. They say if the marriage were concluded we should be obliged to send the princess directly to Scotland, in which case they fear the King of Scotland would not wait, but injure her and endanger her health.

It was Henry's belief that if his mother and wife had their way, James would have to wait for his bride for almost a decade, which might well be a challenge for such a young and virile ruler, who had already fathered at least two illegitimate children (with his former mistress Marion Boyd) and would almost certainly be soon thinking about producing some legitimate heirs to his throne.

Negotiations for the Scottish match were still in their infancy (not least because James was still intent on marrying the reputedly very beautiful Infanta Maria at this point) when the Tudor court went to Sheen Palace in December 1497 to enjoy their traditional annual Christmas celebrations. The royal children were brought from their nursery for the occasion and would often have been seen during the festivities, when the advent fast was broken with days of feasting and dancing. Unlike modern children, Tudor offspring had to wait until New Year's Day for the distribution of presents, which might include gold or silver plate for their dinner table, costly fabrics to make their clothes for the coming year, furs, richly illustrated books and sporting equipment like velvet covered saddles. Despite his much later reputation as a royal miser, Henry VII was a generous husband and father and showered gifts and treats upon his wife and children, ensuring that their chambers were sumptuously furnished, that they were splendidly dressed, and that everything they owned was the very best that money could buy. As his eldest daughter, Margaret did particularly well and the royal records show that she was extremely well dressed in gowns of silk, velvet and brocade, trimmed with the finest lace and furs and accessorised with jewels, leather shoes and pretty hoods. Although it was her ultimate duty to increase the prestige of the young Tudor dynasty by marrying well and anchoring them even further into the network of European royalty that had been intermarrying (and feuding) for generations, at home she was also expected to act as an ambassadress for the family by looking and acting every inch the princess. It was particularly important to King Henry that his family and court should look the part and be unquestionably regal in every way – although he never doubted for an instant his right to the throne, he knew that others questioned his legitimacy to rule and that in some quarters he would always be considered a usurper. His children were therefore never allowed to forget their royal status and encouraged to think themselves innately superior to their peers – which makes one wonder what he would have made of the later marital escapades of all three of his surviving children, all of whom ended up echoing their grandfather Edward IV and making distinctly unremarkable matches with commoners. I think we can safely assume that Henry VII would have been appalled by this lese-majesté.

However, the scandalous matrimonial adventures of his children were far in the future at the end of 1497 as the royal court gathered in magnificent Sheen Palace to celebrate the passing of what had been a fairly lacklustre year. Sprawling along one of the Thames' banks, Sheen had been one of the royal family's favourite residences ever since it was renovated by Henry V in 1414 and had especially happy associations for Queen Elizabeth, whose mother had loved it so much that she made it her primary residence. However, the queen's childhood memories literally went up in flames on the night of 23 December when a fire broke out in her husband's private rooms and rapidly spread through the building, reducing most of it to cinders. The queen and royal children, including 8-year-old Margaret, who was carried out by her nursemaid, were evacuated from their chambers soon after the alarm was raised, but the king's escape was rather more hair-raising as he was forced to sprint down his gallery, which collapsed behind him moments later. The fire raged for several hours, causing huge amounts of damage and destroying precious art works, tapestries, cloth-of-gold bed-hangings and even some of the crown jewels in the process.

It was a serious blow to Queen Elizabeth, but her husband, who obviously did not share her fond associations with the various royal palaces, and may well even have resented them as a reminder of his relative lack of familiarity with his own kingdom, saw the disaster as an opportunity to replace it with a palace of his own creation. It was the first major building project undertaken by the Tudor dynasty and King Henry saw it as an chance to impose his own tastes, which had been honed during his intermittent years of exile on the continent, including a brief period at the famously magnificent French court. Keen as always to promote the legitimacy of his family, the rebuilding of the old palace was also an important exercise in propaganda as it gave him the perfect opportunity to create a palace that would be, he felt, entirely worthy of himself and his heirs and to that end it's not surprising that he also took the opportunity to rename it Richmond Palace, in honour of his old title of Earl of Richmond.

Richmond Palace would be King Henry's pet project over the next few years as he transformed the rubble and fire-blackened walls of old Sheen Palace into one of the most lovely royal residences in Europe. No expense was spared, either on the red-brick exterior with its hundreds of decorative turrets and chimneys and glittering bay windows, or the opulent interior which was furnished with the finest goods that English tradesmen and Henry's many contacts in the trading capitals of the known world could supply, such as tapestries to replace the ones lost in the fire, statues, paintings and ornate, jewel-encrusted plate for the table and a beautiful new chapel. The gardens were also a source of constant admiration to visitors, who went away enraptured by the beautifully arranged flowerbeds, artful topiary hedges and wonderful fountains. Just in case any visitors were in danger of forgetting whose palace this was, every possible surface was covered with the red roses of Lancaster and other symbols and mottos associated with the Tudor dynasty, while King Henry's statue was by far the largest and most prominent of the series of sculptures depicting various kings of England, which stood in alcoves in the new great hall.

Everything in Richmond Palace was brand new – from the shiny window panes to the state-of-the-art early-modern plumbing, but thanks to Henry's own innate good taste, it did not attract the same mockery that a more obviously parvenu effort might have done; instead it was universally admired and hailed as a paradise on earth by more than one foreign visitor. As Henry's young family grew up and negotiations for their future marriages gathered pace, it was of paramount importance to him that these weddings and other celebrations should have a worthy backdrop that proclaimed the prestige of the Tudor family for all the world to see. The first and most magnificent of these celebrations would, he hoped, be the long anticipated marriage of his eldest son Prince Arthur to the Spanish Infanta Catalina, but it's likely that right from the start he was also thinking ahead to the potential wedding of his eldest daughter Margaret and James of Scotland.

Despite the fact that she was the king's eldest daughter, there is precious little mention of Margaret in the official records of this time and so we have no real idea what she was like other than that in her father's opinion she was 'so delicate and female [weak] that she must be married much later than other young ladies' – a view with which the Spanish Ambassador to Scotland, Pedro de Ayala concurred, informing his masters that she was indeed 'very young, and very small for her years'. The art of portraiture was still in its infancy so, unlike the daughters of her Stuart, Georgian and Victorian descendants, there are no known portraits of Margaret as a child, although her few later portraits would suggest that she was pretty, with strong features, a sturdy build and the family red hair. Her future husband, on the other hand, was described at very great length by Pedro de Ayala in a missive to his masters Isabel and Ferdinand, who were clearly curious to know more about the Scottish king who was keen to marry one of their daughters. 'He is of noble stature, neither tall nor short, and as handsome in complexion and shape as a man can be,' Don Pedro reported back admiringly.

> His address is very agreeable. He speaks the following foreign languages; Latin, very well; French, German, Flemish, Italian, and Spanish; Spanish as well as the Marquis, but he pronounces

it more distinctly. He likes, very much, to receive Spanish letters. His own Scotch language is as different from English as Aragonese from Castilian. The king speaks, besides, the language of the savages who live in some parts of Scotland and on the islands. It is as different from Scotch as Biscayan is from Castilian. His knowledge of languages is wonderful. He is well read in the Bible and in some other devout books. He is a good historian. He has read many Latin and French histories, and profited by them, as he has a very good memory. He never cuts his hair or his beard. It becomes him very well.

He went on to describe James's character, with obvious emphasis on his piety and personal courage, both of which were considered highly desirable traits for any early modern monarch.

He fears God, and observes all the precepts of the Church. He does not eat meat on Wednesdays and Fridays. He would not ride on Sundays for any consideration, not even to mass. He says all his prayers. Before transacting any business he hears two masses. After mass he has a cantata sung, during which he sometimes despatches very urgent business. He gives alms liberally, but is a severe judge, especially in the case of murderers. He has a great predilection for priests, and receives advice from them, especially from the Friars Observant, with whom he confesses. Rarely, even in joking, a word escapes him that is not the truth. He prides himself much upon it, and says it does not seem to him well for kings to swear their treaties as they do now. The oath of a king should be his royal word, as was the case in bygone ages. He is neither prodigal nor avaricious, but liberal when occasion requires. He is courageous, even more so than a king should be. I am a good witness of it. I have seen him often undertake most dangerous things in the last wars. I sometimes clung to his skirts, and succeeded in keeping him back. On such occasions he does not take the least care of himself. He is not a good captain, because he begins to fight before he has given his orders. He said to me that his subjects serve him with their persons and goods, in just and unjust quarrels, exactly as he likes, and that, therefore, he does not think it right to begin any warlike undertaking without being himself the first in danger. His deeds are as good as his words. For this reason, and because he is a very humane prince, he is much loved. He is active, and works hard. When he is not at war he hunts in the mountains. I tell your Highnesses the truth when I say that God has worked a miracle in him, for I have never seen a man so temperate in eating and drinking out of Spain. Indeed such a thing seems to be superhuman in these countries. He lends a willing ear to his counsellors, and decides nothing without asking them; but in great matters he acts according to his own judgment, and, in my opinion, he generally makes a right decision. I recognise him perfectly in the conclusion of the last peace, which was made against the wishes of the majority in his kingdom.

Don Pedro added:

I can say with truth that he esteems himself as much as though he were Lord of the world. He loves war so much that I fear, judging by the provocation he receives, the peace will not last long. War is profitable to him and to the country.

He not only talked about James, but also lengthily described the assets, national morale and character of Scotland and its people, informing the Spanish monarchs that Scotland,

is large. Your Highnesses know that these kingdoms form an island. Judging by what I have read in books and seen on maps, and also by my own experience, I should think that both kingdoms are of equal extent. In the same proportion that England is longer than Scotland, Scotland is wider than England; thus the quantity of land is the same. Neither is the quality very different in the two countries, but the Scotch are not industrious, and the people are poor. They spend all their time in wars, and when there is no war they fight with one another. It must, however, be observed that since the present king succeeded to the throne they do not dare to quarrel so much with one another as formerly, especially since he came of age. They have learnt by experience that he executes the law without respect to rich or poor. I am told that Scotland has improved so much during his reign that it is worth three times more now than formerly, on account of foreigners having come to the country, and taught them how to live.

The Scottish people he described as 'handsome', adding that:

They like foreigners so much that they dispute with one another as to who shall have and treat a foreigner in his house. They are vain and ostentatious by nature. They spend all they have to keep up appearances. They are as well dressed as it is possible to be in such a country as that in which they live. They are courageous, strong, quick, and agile. They are envious to excess.

He was especially complimentary about the women of Scotland:

The women are courteous in the extreme. I mention this because they are really honest, though very bold. They are absolute mistresses of their houses, and even of their husbands, in all things concerning the administration of their property, income as well as expenditure. They are very graceful and handsome women. They dress much better than here [England], and especially as regards the head-dress, which is, I think, the handsomest in the world.

In summary, neither the Spanish or English monarchs needed to fear sending their precious daughters to the northern, and allegedly rather inhospitable, kingdom of Scotland. In a candid conversation with Don Pedro de Ayala, King Henry appeared 'content and cheerful' at the prospect of making a match between his daughter and James, but admitted that he was possibly the only person in favour of the marriage as his wife and mother were concerned about the age gap between the two. In his view, as it might well be another eight years before the physically immature Margaret was ready for marriage, it would be better for James to instead pursue his preferred match with the 16-year-old Infanta Maria, the only unspoken-for daughter of Ferdinand and Isabel, which would still act as an alliance between the three nations due to her younger sister Catalina's betrothal to Prince Arthur. Here again though, Henry admitted that the match would be an unpopular one – this time with his people, who would, he feared, be jealous and resent the Scottish king for making a marriage of equal grandeur to that contracted by the English heir to the throne.

The death in childbirth of Infanta Maria's elder sister Isabel, Queen of Portugal, in August 1498, however, effectively put paid to any hope of a Spanish match for Scotland as her parents immediately determined that the Portuguese alliance was far too important to lose and instantly pledged to maintain it by marrying Maria, whom they were still hoping to marry to the newly single Louis XII of France, to her sister's widower as soon as a decent period of mourning had elapsed. This was a serious blow for James, who had set his heart on a Spanish match, but he put a brave face on things and immediately started buttering up Henry in the hopes of securing Princess Margaret instead. However, while James's dreams of marrying a beautiful Spanish princess were coming to nothing, Henry, who may well have been rather more piqued than he was letting on by his Scottish neighbour's lack of interest in Margaret as a prospective bride, had been quietly considering other matches for his eldest daughter. It's unlikely that he ever seriously considered her other suitors, but the missives of the Venetian Ambassador reveal that Henry was at one point considering a match between Margaret and Jacques de Rohan, the eldest son of Jean II, Vicomte de Rohan, who was the male heir presumptive to the Duchy of Brittany should Duchesse Anne, who had recently pipped Infanta Maria to the post and married Louis XII of France, die without any children of her own.

Another contender, although never a serious one, was Massimiliano Sforza, eldest son of Ludovico Sforza, Duke of Milan, who sent a delegation to England in 1498 in order to try to acquire one of Henry's two daughters for his heir – rather ungallantly stating that he did not mind which one he got so long as she came with the assurance of English support against Louis XII's threat to seize Milan for himself. A much more significant contender, however, was James of Scotland's 17-year-old first cousin Prince Christian, the eldest son of the King of Denmark, who could be a very useful ally to the English. Luckily for James though, the Danish match fell through almost as soon as it was suggested and on 11 September 1498, King Henry admitted defeat and instructed one of his most trusted advisors and diplomats Richard Foxe, Bishop of Durham, to officially begin negotiations for Margaret's marriage to the King of Scotland.

Chapter 4

Wedding Bells 1499–1502

Although the marriage of the eldest Tudor princess was very far from being an insignificant matter either for her family or the nation as a whole, it would be very fair to say that it was almost completely outshone by the extravagant wedding plans being made for her elder brother Arthur, Prince of Wales and the Infanta Catalina of Aragon. For Henry VII, pulling off this match with Spain, one of the greatest super powers in the known world at the end of the fifteenth century, was a massive coup and one that he had been hoping for ever since he had seized the English throne in 1485. Catalina would bring with her not just a closer relationship to the monarchs of Castile and Aragon, but also a vast dowry of 200,000 escudos (roughly equivalent to £100,000, which was an enormous amount of money at the end of the fifteenth century), which would make a significant difference to the royal coffers and enable the newly married couple to live in considerable style. Also of importance to Henry was the fact that almost eighty years had passed since Henry V had married the French princess Catherine de Valois in the wake of Agincourt in 1420, and that this was the last time that a foreign princess had married either the English monarch or his heir. Although contracting a more home grown match to Elizabeth of York had been of massive benefit to him, Henry still believed that it gave a nation a huge boost in prestige and importance on the world stage to be seen making marriages with other world powers and at the time, the daughters of Ferdinand and Isabel were the greatest prizes of all so he was particularly pleased to be able to acquire one for his family.

The young couple had been considered formally betrothed since February 1497 but the proxy wedding did not take place until 19 May 1499. It was a small, one might even say intimate, affair held in the chapel of Tickenhill Manor near Bewdley in Worcestershire, one of Prince Arthur's main residences. As the Infanta had yet to leave Spain, the Spanish Ambassador Roderigo de Puebla stood in for the bride during the ceremony. From now on Arthur and 13-year-old Catalina could consider themselves legally bound in marriage and would refer to each other as 'my dearest spouse', and other such endearments in their correspondence. However, another two years would pass before they would meet in person and begin their actual married life. In the meantime, King Henry busied himself preparing for Catalina's arrival, which primarily involved completing work on the new Richmond Palace, which he planned to make the centrepiece of the celebrations.

Henry was perhaps even more impatient to meet Catalina than his son was and took an interest in every detail of her reception and future life in his country, even down to specifying that the ladies of her entourage should be as attractive as possible. His wife was rather less involved in the preparations but then she had given birth to their third son, Prince Edmund, who was styled Duke of Somerset, on 21 February 1499 and was therefore somewhat preoccupied for much of the year. The rest of the royal children were no doubt very pleased to have another baby in their midst and we catch a lovely glimpse of the 7-month-old Prince Edmund in his nurse's arms in the noted Renaissance scholar Erasmus's well known description of his visit to the royal nurseries at Eltham in September of that year. Erasmus, who was already something of a celebrity in scholarly circles, had been taken to Eltham by his friend Thomas More and was surprised to find the whole household waiting to greet them with the 8-year-old Prince Henry, Duke of York at the centre, while his sisters 9-year-old Margaret and 3-year-old Mary stood beside him, attended by their new governess Joan Vaux, Lady Guildford. Unfortunately, Erasmus was so struck by the nascent intelligence and charisma of the young Prince Henry that he spared barely a glance for his two sisters other than to note their presence at the meeting.

Although Ferdinand and Isabel had originally informed Henry that they would be dispatching their daughter to him once she had reached her fourteenth birthday in December, they decided to postpone when another pretender, this time claiming to be the queen's hapless cousin the Earl of Warwick, made an appearance and was swiftly captured and executed before he could garner any popular support. Edward Plantagenet, the real Earl of Warwick had been imprisoned in the Tower for fourteen years, having been deposited there at the age of 10 after his uncle Richard III's defeat at Bosworth. The only son of Richard's scapegrace brother George, Duke of Clarence, he was considered by some to be the true male Yorkist heir to the throne with a far stronger claim than that of King Henry. To date, Henry had actually treated him very well, although he had obviously balked at letting the boy leave the Tower and have any sort of life of his own. However, this was the second time that someone had come forward claiming to be the earl and understandably, Ferdinand and Isabel were beginning to fear that one day someone might just let the real thing out of the Tower and help him take the throne – which would not bode well for the future prospects of their daughter Catalina. Henry was dismayed but not in the least bit surprised when Ferdinand of Aragon intimated that there was no possible way that his daughter could set foot in England until Warwick had been neutralised.

It might have been easier to have the unfortunate young earl, who was said to be a simpleton but was more than likely just very naïve due to the fact that he'd spent more than half of his life inside the Tower, quietly murdered, but if Henry had learned anything during his fourteen years on the throne it was that boys who vanished inside the thick stone walls of the tower had a tendency to 'reappear' at the most inopportune moments and if Warwick was to be killed off, then it would have to be done publicly and with every appearance of legal process. To this end, Warwick was allowed to consort with Perkin Warbeck, who had been imprisoned in the Tower after his abortive attempt to escape from Henry's custody. Keen to reassure Ferdinand and Isabella of the unassailability of his throne, and no doubt thinking that he might as well kill two annoying birds with one decisive stone, Henry either let nature run its course or endeavoured to somehow prod the two undoubtedly restless young men towards treason. Either way, they quickly came up with a plan to escape together, were swiftly captured, tried and then executed at the end of November. Having confessed to his humble origins, Warbeck was hanged at Tyburn, while Warwick, as befitted his rank as a cousin of the queen, was beheaded on Tower Hill. Besides his wife Catherine, who would remain at court in the service of Queen Elizabeth, few people shed tears for Perkin Warbeck but it was generally felt that the execution of the Earl of Warwick had cast something of a pall over the forthcoming wedding and indeed Catalina herself, by then known as Catherine and married to Arthur's brother Henry, would later say that her first marriage had been 'made in blood' and, as a result, cursed from the outset.

In January 1500, now satisfied that the Tudor throne had been secured against any immediate threat from real and imaginary Plantagenet princelings, Ferdinand and Isabel informed King Henry that they were happy to send their daughter to England as soon as Prince Arthur had reached the age of 15 on 20 September 1501. This was good news for the Tudors as it meant that all the long years of negotiation, haggling and stress were finally coming to an end. However, their celebratory mood was to be short lived as the sweating sickness epidemic that had stricken the nation since the previous summer became increasingly ferocious, to the extent that King Henry, who had himself just recovered from a bout of illness that had by all accounts left him virtually at death's door, became seriously alarmed for the wellbeing of his family. Taking swift action, he packed the four youngest children off to the royal manor at Hatfield and carried his wife Elizabeth off to Calais at the start of May for a sojourn that would eventually last for over a month. As is typical of Henry, it was not just the relatively salubrious air in Calais that attracted him across the Channel but also the proximity to the Habsburg-controlled Netherlands, which were ruled over by Archduke Philip, the spoiled, handsome son of the Emperor Maximilian I. Perhaps of equal interest to Henry and Elizabeth was Philip's beautiful but slightly unstable wife, Juana of Castile, the eldest sister of their as yet unseen daughter-in-law Catalina.

The two royal couples immediately hit it off during their meeting in Calais, with King Henry clearly being impressed by Juana's golden-haired loveliness, intelligence and wit, and after making the usual grand, but ultimately meaningless, protestations of eternal friendship they decided to cement their new understanding by agreeing to marry Philip's baby son Charles to the Princess Mary, while the eldest Habsburg Archduchess, Eleanor, would be betrothed to Prince Henry. The royal couple had every reason to feel triumphant as they returned home to England – only for their buoyant mood to be punctured when news arrived that their youngest child, Prince Edmund, who was not quite 16 months old, had died a few days earlier. Like his sister Elizabeth, the child was accorded a lavish state funeral in Westminster Abbey which his elder siblings, who now had to adjust to his disappearance from the royal nurseries, almost certainly did not attend.

It had been a stressful, difficult couple of years for King Henry and his family but as the first year of the sixteenth century drew to a close, they at least had much to look forward to in the coming twelve months – not least the long awaited and much anticipated arrival of the Infanta Catalina, who would be known as Catherine in her new, adopted country. It was to be the first major public celebration since the coronation of Queen Elizabeth in November 1487 and Henry was determined to make the most of this opportunity to showcase the wealth, prestige and strength of the Tudor dynasty. He had weathered several storms, both personal and political, during the sixteen years that had passed since he claimed the crown on Bosworth Field, and had achieved with aplomb the difficult task of uniting and healing a nation that had been ripped apart by civil war. England was more peaceful than it had been for decades and was rapidly growing in prosperity under Tudor rule. Henry had every reason to be proud of his achievements, both as a king and the head of a new royal dynasty; the arrival of the Spanish Infanta, who personified just how far he and his country had come since 1485, gave him the perfect excuse to celebrate. Vast amounts of money were being spent on his new Richmond Palace, which was being literally raised, phoenix-like, from the ashes of the destroyed Sheen Palace, while yet more enormous sums were being put aside for the wedding and its accompanying weeks of festivities. The Infanta left Spain for the last time on 27 September 1501 and after a stormy and eventful journey, arrived at Plymouth in Devon on 2 October. She had originally been expected to land in Southampton, which was much closer to the capital, but the terrible weather had forced her to land much sooner than expected. Luckily for Catherine, her arrival was not entirely out of the blue and there was a large crowd and committee of local nobility waiting to welcome her to England before she embarked on a slow progress across the country to meet her future husband and, perhaps more importantly, his father, who was full of impatience to see her.

Whereas Henry and his sons met Catherine during her slow progress to London, the ladies of the royal family did not set eyes upon her until 12 November when she made her formal state entry into the capital at the end of her journey through southern England. The young Spanish princess, who shared the same auburn hair and pale colouring as her husband and his siblings, was the central focus of an elaborate mounted procession that wound through the streets of London, watched by a vast, cheering crowd. Queen Elizabeth, Lady Margaret Beaufort and the princesses watched some of the procession from an upstairs chamber in the Cornhill house of a wealthy haberdasher, William Geoffrey, and were doubtless much struck and very relieved by the Infanta's prettiness, lovely clothes and pleasingly friendly manner. However, they did not actually meet her until the following afternoon when Catherine was taken to the great riverside mansion of Baynard's Castle in order to be introduced to her new mother-in-law as well as the other ladies of the family, including the Princesses Margaret and Mary. Once all the formalities were at an end, the ladies and their entourage spent the evening having fun and dancing, albeit somewhat hampered by some language barriers on both sides as Catherine had not yet mastered the English tongue, before the Spanish princess departed to prepare for her wedding the next day. While their elder brother, Prince Arthur, was obviously the main star of the show, his younger siblings were also keen to be involved in the public celebrations for the royal wedding. The 9-year-old Prince Henry had a prominent role in the ceremony; he had the enviable job of standing in for her own absent male relatives and escorting the Infanta, who was dressed in white and gold satin and had an exquisite coronet and lace mantilla covering her long auburn hair, up the aisle of St Paul's Cathedral before she married his brother in front of a vast congregation comprising all the great and good of the nation. Meanwhile, King Henry, Queen Elizabeth and Lady Margaret Beaufort watched the ceremony from behind a specially constructed grille placed close to the altar, which hid them from view and meant that the young couple would be the centre of attention.

It is not known if Princesses Margaret and Mary were present at the ceremony, but as the royal accounts make it clear that both girls were provided with rich new wardrobes for the occasion, with Margaret receiving a tawny cloth-of-gold gown trimmed with royal ermine, a purple velvet gown and kirtles made from tawny and russet satin along with black and crimson velvet French style hoods to cover her hair, it's probable that they too were present. As Margaret was now nearly 12-years-old, it is likely that she was considered old enough to at least witness the ceremony if not actually take part – the great honour of carrying the Infanta's long train as she walked up the aisle fell to the groom's aunt Princess Cecily of York, who had performed the same office at the coronation of her sister Queen Elizabeth, rather than either of his sisters. Margaret definitely took part in the following celebrations, which involved the usual magnificent tournaments and banquets, though, even leading the dancing one evening with her brother Henry as partner – at least one witness admiringly recorded the young Duke of York's vigorous dancing, which left him so overheated that he was forced to remove his coat, but of his sister's dancing skills, there was no mention. On another occasion, the king and queen presided over an extraordinary banquet in Westminster Palace, where Margaret and Henry were seated on the same table as their brother Arthur (his new bride had the place of honour at his father's table) before enjoying an evening of extravagant entertainments in Westminster Hall. Their new sister-in-law Catherine, Princess of Wales, briefly spent time with the royal family before travelling to Ludlow Castle in Herefordshire, where her husband presided over his own court, in late December. It's not known what the three princesses thought of each other, especially as Catherine was four years older than her eldest sister-in-law Margaret – which may not seem like much of a gap nowadays but would have constituted a huge gulf in the sixteenth century, when one was a married lady with her own household and the other was still technically a resident of the royal nurseries.

The sophisticated, intelligent and well-read Catherine may also have found little common ground with Margaret, who lacked the intellectual gifts of her siblings and seems to have been an unwilling scholar. However, as we know from their later friendship, and more particularly the loyalty that Princess Mary displayed towards Catherine when her position was being usurped by Anne Boleyn in the 1530s, it seems likely that she found the youngest Tudor princess to be more congenial company than the elder.

Whatever she thought of her new sister-in-law, Margaret must have been paying close attention to the wedding preparations and ensuing celebrations as she fully expected to be married herself before long – an assumption strengthened by the arrival on 14 November of envoys from the Scottish court, who had been despatched to oversee the final arrangements of the betrothal. The negotiations for her own marriage had been held up in the middle of 1500 by the usual squabbling about money, with King James demanding that her father provide a dowry equal to that which he would have received from Ferdinand and Isabella should he have married the Infanta Maria. However, Henry was naturally unwilling to part with such an enormous sum and instead offered twice the amount that his father-in-law Edward IV had offered during the short-lived negotiations to marry his daughter Princess Cecily to James over twenty years earlier. James was unimpressed as this was less than half of what he had asked for and so there had briefly existed a stalemate between the two. Like Henry a year earlier, James then began to look elsewhere for a bride, intimating his interest in Emperor Maximilian's only daughter, the recently widowed Margaret, Princess of the Asturias, and also in Louis XII's niece Germaine de Foix, the daughter of his sister Marie d'Orléans, Comtesse d'Étampes – a match that was much less prestigious than the others but would have brought him the huge benefit of being linked to the King of France (Mademoiselle de Foix would later become the second wife of Ferdinand of Aragon after his first wife Isabella of Castile died in November 1504). Nonetheless, the impasse between England and Scotland came to an end in June 1500, when James, who must have known all along that he would never have a better chance than this match with England, agreed to Henry's terms and the matter was settled. Ferdinand and Isabella, who had taken a great interest in the situation, and may even have intervened to bring about the result they had wanted all along, expressed themselves pleased with the arrangement, even going so far as to assure King Henry that they were 'as much, and more, pleased with it than if he [James] had been going to marry their own daughter'. Which was probably not far from the truth, all things considered.

The arrival of the Scottish envoys, headed by the Archbishop of Glasgow, the 1st Earl of Bothwell and the postulate Bishop of Moray, clearly signified that the match was on track to happen very soon and as Margaret appeared alongside her family at the various wedding celebrations that autumn, she must have been aware that the Scottish visitors were taking careful note of her appearance and behaviour in order to report back to their master, King James. There may also have been at least one private meeting, heavily chaperoned by either her mother or grandmother of course, between Margaret and the envoys, so they could take the opportunity to speak to her in person. Either way, the Scottish were pleased with what they saw and undoubtedly extremely impressed by the lavish pageantry that marked Prince Arthur's wedding and the magnificence of the Tudor palaces, particularly Richmond, where the court retreated to spend Christmas that year. It was at Richmond Palace that the treaty of marriage between England and Scotland was concluded on 24 January 1502 in the presence of King Henry and Queen Elizabeth, who agreed to send Margaret to Scotland with a dowry of £30,000 (£10,000 in English money, which was equivalent to roughly £6 million in today's money), one third of which would accompany her to Scotland while the other two thirds would be paid after two years. In return, James agreed to bestow upon their daughter the rich jointure lands traditionally given to the queens of Scotland – most significantly Linlithgow Palace and Stirling Castle near Edinburgh, which would be her main residences, as well as Methven Castle and Doune Castle. She would also receive the rents and income from a variety of smaller properties, including Ettrick Forest in the Scottish Borders as well as the Earldoms of March and Menteith and the Lairdships of Cockburnspath, Dunbar, Methven and Doune. James also undertook to pay most of the expenses of Margaret's wardrobe, stables and household, while her father, almost certainly motivated by concern that she would be lonely so far from home, agreed to supply her with a sizeable entourage of twenty-four English servants. In monetary terms, Margaret's annual income would amount to around £2,000 (about £1 million in today's money) with about £300 (about £175,000 in today's money) being for her own personal use once all other expenses had been met.

At the same time, the Scottish and English also signed two other treaties. The first of which promised perpetual peace and friendship between the two bordering nations and had been promoted by a whole host of other European powers such as Ferdinand and Isabella of Spain, Louis XII of France and the Emperor Maximilian, all of whom were keen to see an end to the tiresome bickering between England and Scotland. The second treaty dealt more specifically with the issue of fairly policing the contentious border area that lay between the two nations, where pillaging, petty theft and other civil disorder was rife. According to the terms of this third agreement, there would be increased supervision of the area and a new fairer legislative system put in place, with miscreants from both nations being tried in a more orderly manner by a properly appointed judge and jury of citizens drawn from both sides of the border. The thousands of law-abiding people who lived in the afflicted areas must have welcomed this new accord between England and Scotland; there was no doubt that border raids had made their lives miserable and led to a great deal of ill feeling and justified suspicion between the two nations.

The official ceremony of betrothal took place the following day. The highest ranking churchmen and nobility in the land as well as diplomats from Spain, France, Venice and the Vatican gathered together to hear Mass and then a sermon delivered by the Bishop of Chichester in the beautiful new royal chapel, before processing to the queen's Great Chamber, which had been specially decorated with Tudor roses and Scottish thistles for the occasion. There, King Henry and Queen Elizabeth, the proud parents, seated themselves beneath their cloth of estate, while their younger children, Prince Henry and Princess Mary sat on gilded stools before them. Lady Margaret Beaufort, the bride's grandmother, was curiously absent – perhaps because of ill health as it's unlikely that she would have willingly missed such an important occasion for her family. Margaret, alone, stood in the centre of the room – for once the star of the show and cynosure of all eyes as the Archbishop of Glasgow asked her if she knew of any impediment to her marriage and if she gave herself freely and without compulsion to marriage with the Scottish king. 'If it please my lord and father the king, and my lady and mother, the Queen,' was the demure reply. Once the royal couple had signified their permission for the marriage to go ahead and given their daughter their blessing as she entered this new phase in her life, the ceremony was able to continue. Standing in for King James, who remained in Scotland, was one of his favourites, the handsome but slightly raffish Patrick Hepburn, 1st Earl of Bothwell, who acted as proxy during the ceremony of betrothal, wearing a splendid cloth-of-gold outfit for the occasion. Margaret's small young voice might well have proved difficult to hear in the vast, crowded chamber but the deed was done, her fate was sealed and she was considered as good as married to King James as soon as she said the words that everyone had been waiting to hear ever since negotiations between Scotland and England had opened all those years earlier.

> I, Margaret, the first begotten daughter of the right excellent, right high and mighty Prince and Princess, Henry by the grace of God, King of England and Elizabeth, queen of the same, wittingly and of deliberate mind having twelve years complete in age in the month of November last be past, contract matrimony with the right excellent, right high and mighty Prince, James, King of Scotland, the person of whom Patrick, Earl of Bothwell, is procurator; and take the said James, King of Scotland, unto and for my husband and spouse and all other for him forsake, during his and mine lives natural; and thereto I plight and give to him, in your person as procurator aforesaid, my faith and troth.

After the betrothal ceremony was over, King Henry took the Scottish notables and other gentlemen off for a lively banquet in his own chambers, while his wife Elizabeth and daughter went to dinner together hand-in-hand, and then ate from the same plate, to signify that they were now both married ladies and of equal rank. After dinner, there was jousting and a celebratory banquet, while up the Thames in London, great bonfires were built in the streets and free wine was handed out to the populace so that they too could celebrate the betrothal of the eldest Tudor princess. The following day, there were still more jousts, during which a handsome newcomer Charles Brandon, whose father had been killed by Richard III himself while bearing King Henry's standard at Bosworth and was therefore much favoured by the royal family, caught the attention of several of the court ladies when he came third in the competition. As was to be expected, Margaret had the honour of presenting the prizes for the jousting, after which there was a delightful pageant or masque in the palace's great hall, followed by yet another lengthy banquet and entertainments that went on until late in the night.

Although the celebrations were definitely more low-key than those that had recently marked the marriage of Prince Arthur and Catherine of Aragon, King Henry was clearly keen to put on a good show on his daughter's behalf, not just to show his pleasure at her match but also to show off in front of the visiting Scots, who would be reporting every detail back to their master and would also be sent back with rich presents of gold and silver plate, clothes and money. For Margaret, who had been so often ignored in favour of her more charismatic elder brothers or prettier younger sister, this was a rare opportunity to be the centre of attention and it's likely that she made the most of the experience. Although her family were very clear that she would not be departing for Scotland for quite some time, in the meantime she was to be treated like a queen with her own household and opulent apartments in the royal palaces, complete with the Scottish cloth of estate over her chair when she dined or greeted visitors. Although to some extent this marked Margaret's escape from the nursery, her lessons would still have continued and she would have found her life almost as restricted as it had always been – the relative freedom of older married ladies such as her mother would not be accorded to her until she had joined her husband in Scotland and taken charge of her own household.

The international community were relieved and pleased to hear that Scotland and England had finally come to an agreement after so many years of uncertainty. On 15 April 1502, Ferdinand and Isabella wrote to their Ambassador in England in order to express their pleasure that the marriage treaty had at last been concluded to the satisfaction of all parties and the couple duly betrothed. The Spanish monarchs had taken a great interest in the match, as they believed that it would significantly increase the security of their daughter Catherine if her adoptive country England was at peace with its neighbour Scotland. However, by the time their congratulations had arrived in London, Prince Arthur was dead at just fifteen-years-old, their daughter was a widow mere months after she had been married amid such enormous pageantry, the English court was in mourning and everything had changed forever.

Chapter 5

The Worst of Times 1502–1503

It started with a fever, as these sudden tragic sixteenth-century deaths all too often did, and although the young prince was not initially despaired of, his condition had nonetheless rapidly worsened before he passed away on 2 April 1502. It took two days for the sad tale of Prince Arthur's death to reach London and we can only imagine how frightened the unfortunate messenger felt as he got closer to the capital, knowing that he carried with him the worst possible news. Although Prince Arthur's poor health had been common knowledge for quite some time, it was still a terrible shock for King Henry when he was woken in the dark of night by his confessor, who reminded him of Job's words, 'Si bona de manu Dei suscipimus, mala autem quare non sustineamus?' ('If we receive good things from the hands of God, why should we not also endure evil things?') before gently informing him that his eldest son was dead.

Henry's grief was dreadful to behold, as was that of his wife Elizabeth, whom he immediately summoned to his chambers so that he could break the news himself. Elizabeth had endured the premature loss of her parents, brothers, two small children and other close family members with her usual grace and composure, but the death of her eldest son proved too much for her and after leaving her husband she collapsed in her chambers, at which point King Henry hastened to comfort her and they both wept together for their loss. It makes for touching reading but even in the midst of their great personal pain, the royal couple could not forget that as well as grieving parents, they were also ruling monarchs with a responsibility both to the crown and also their people. They consoled each other with the fact that they still had another son, Prince Henry, who was now heir to the throne, and also two daughters, Margaret and Mary – although the girls couldn't be considered much of a comfort at a time when no woman had yet been crowned Queen of England and ruled in her own right. Although very fond of their daughters, Henry and Elizabeth were both aware that if anything happened to their son

Prince Henry, the Tudor dynasty they had worked so hard to create would quickly find itself teetering on the edge of disaster, if not outright extinction.

If anything had happened to Prince Henry at this time then his sister Margaret's marriage to James of Scotland could have posed an interesting problem for their father, King Henry. With two hale and hearty male heirs ready to take over after his death, it's unlikely that there was any serious discussion about Margaret's potential inheritance during her marriage negotiations as it must have seemed unlikely that her brothers should die before her, or without at least producing male heirs of their own; that had all changed now that there was just one male heir standing between Margaret and the throne. Indeed, there is evidence that the subject was at least vaguely raised by King Henry's council at one point and he cheerfully, and rather prophetically, replied:

> Supposing, which God forbid, that all my male progeny should become extinct and the kingdom devolve by law to Margaret's heirs, will England be damaged thereby, or rather benefited? For since the less becomes subservient to the greater, the accession will be that of Scotland to England, not of England to Scotland.

Clearly Henry anticipated a situation rather like the one that had occurred when his ancestor, William of Normandy, had seized England in the eleventh century or, more prophetically, the events that followed the death of his granddaughter Elizabeth I almost exactly a century later in March 1603 when the throne was indeed claimed by Margaret's male descendant, her great grandson James VI of Scotland. Although King Henry was almost certainly determined to pass the throne to his sole remaining son and not allow it to slip into the hands of the Scots, he might have consoled himself with the fact that he could do much worse – it certainly would never have occurred to him that Margaret would be capable of reigning in her own right, in which case the character of her husband was key to the success of her reign as it would have been accepted by everyone that he, rather than his wife, would be the true power in the realm. Would the English accept a Scottish king? Very probably – after all they had accepted Henry Tudor in 1487 even though the vast majority of his subjects had no real idea who he was and even less of a clue why he believed he had a right to the throne. Of course, it wouldn't hurt that almost everyone agreed that James of Scotland was the epitome of the sophisticated, intelligent and courageous Renaissance prince and would almost certainly have been a more than capable ruler of England – some might even argue that he would have done a better job than his brother-in-law and great rival, Henry VIII.

Who knows what thoughts were running through King Henry's mind as he comforted his weeping wife in her chambers at Greenwich Palace. However, despite her distress, Elizabeth was quick to grasp that the Tudor succession could not rely on one male heir and took the course of reminding her husband that she was still only 36-years-old and there was every chance they could have more children. She had been desperately ill during her last pregnancy and, as events would prove, should almost certainly have been taking measures not to get pregnant again rather than deliberately trying to have another baby, but with the Tudor throne in potential peril, she probably felt as though she had no choice – and indeed was pregnant again by the end of the following month. In the meantime, there were more pressing matters to deal with, such as Arthur's funeral and the fate of the widowed Catherine, Princess of Wales, who was also ill, although not gravely, and would soon be able to return to London. Unexpectedly, Arthur's body was laid to rest in Worcester Cathedral rather than Westminster Abbey, where his father was already planning the magnificent Lady Chapel that he intended to become the Tudor family mausoleum. The decision to bury him so far away from the capital suggests there was a fear that the illness (still to this day unidentified) that killed him may have been contagious. Although he was being laid to rest on the other side of the country, his grieving parents did everything they could to ensure that his funeral was suitably magnificent and did him every possible honour.

As was traditional, none of the royal family were present at Arthur's internment, but most of his now-dissolved household returned to London afterwards and would have been able to tell his parents and siblings how magnificent the funeral was and how mourned he was by the people he had lived among since childhood. For his 10-year-old brother Henry, the death of Prince Arthur brought about an almost unbelievable but no doubt very welcome change in rank and circumstance as he was elevated from the position of second son to heir. It would have been strange for his two sisters as well – although Arthur had been raised apart from them since early childhood, with the consequence that they didn't see all that much of him, he was still an affectionate and kind-hearted brother and a genuine warmth had existed between him and his younger siblings. He would be greatly missed by all. For his sisters there was also the strangeness of getting used to the fact that the future King of England would not after all be the relatively distant Arthur, who had been kept away from his younger siblings and carefully nurtured and tutored for his glorious destiny, but instead the more familiar Henry, who had been raised alongside them since babyhood. Whereas no one had been in any doubt of Arthur's exalted and privileged status within the Tudor family, they had eaten, squabbled, suffered childhood illnesses, played, laughed and learned alongside Henry right from the start and were familiar with him in a way that, for all their fondness, they could never have been with Arthur. The rivalries and loyalties forged in the royal nurseries would overshadow the three surviving Tudor siblings for the rest of their lives and would have a significant, and not always pleasing, effect on the lives of Henry's sisters – both of whom would be dismayed on more than one occasion by their brother's callous treatment towards them.

True to form, a vast amount of money was spent on the mourning apparel of the royal family and their households. The queen and princesses wore black until the end of the year, with the royal accounts showing that they ordered some new clothes and also thriftily paid to have existing mourning dresses mended and relined. It was an expensive time for the royal coffers as they not only had to pay for mourning clothes for the royal ladies, but also dresses for Margaret's upcoming wedding and her all important trousseau – the expansive wardrobe of rich clothes and accessories that she would take with her to Scotland so that she would look every inch a queen from the moment she crossed the border. We know from the royal accounts that the additional expense caused Queen Elizabeth some financial embarrassment and she was forced to borrow money from her husband in order to make the necessary repayments.

As the year went on, the mourning gradually lightened, with Queen Elizabeth, who loved to indulge her children, buying two new pairs of sarcenet (a light taffeta silk) sleeves, one white and one orange, for Margaret to wear with her black dresses. The orange sarcenet sleeves were a particular favourite and there was much fuss when she accidentally left them at Baynard's Castle and her mother's unfortunate Page of the Robes, Richard Justice, was despatched by boat in order to bring them to her at Westminster Palace. No doubt Elizabeth was feeling especially indulgent towards Margaret as preparations for her wedding gathered pace and she prepared to say goodbye, perhaps forever, to her eldest daughter. Although Margaret was much more fortunate than many princesses, notably her own sister-in-law Catherine of Aragon, in that she was not being sent thousands of miles away from home, there was still an expectation that she would remain in Scotland for the rest of her life and might very well never cross the border and return home again, not even for a visit. It must have been a daunting prospect for a 12-year-old girl, but Margaret had been carefully reared to respect her parents and grandmother, Lady Margaret Beaufort, and would have been content to let them guide her in all things. She may also have been looking forward to escaping the gloomy atmosphere of her father's court, where all the usual festivities had been cancelled in the wake of Arthur's death and her mother spent much of the summer on progress around Wales and the West Country.

Margaret and her sister Mary occupied their time reading devotional books, doubtless recommended by their grandmother who took a keen interest in their spiritual education, and practicing their music – in July, the royal accounts show that Queen Elizabeth had Margaret's lute restrung and there were also payments for the little Queen of Scots' personal minstrel troupe, who played for the court at that year's Christmas celebrations at Richmond Palace.

At the end of January 1503, the heavily pregnant Queen Elizabeth made her way by boat down the Thames to the Tower of London, where she was to celebrate the festival of Candelmas with her husband. The queen had been in an introspective, preoccupied mood ever since the death of her eldest son and had been spending much of her time with her sisters and their families – with particular attention being paid to her sister Catherine, Countess of Devon, and her children, one of whom, 5-year-old Edward, died in July 1502, which brought the two sisters closer in their mutual grief. Once again, the queen's pregnancy was not an easy one and she may have been plagued by anaemia as well as other unpleasant physical symptoms that led her to consult several times with her physicians. The plight of her widowed daughter-in-law Catherine of Aragon was also preying on her mind – the despondent young princess had returned to London, where she took up residence at Durham House on the river, shortly after her husband's death and immediately found herself at the centre of an ugly diplomatic row between her parents, who wanted her either returned to Spain or honourably remarried to the new heir Prince Henry while King Henry had no wish to lose the half of her dowry that was still owed to him.

It was an unpleasant situation for the sensitive and already homesick young Princess to be in and Elizabeth did everything she could to make her welcome at court. And while she consoled the depressed and lonely Catherine, she also had to devote some time to assuaging the fears and apprehensions of her eldest daughter Margaret, who was to leave for

Scotland in the summer of 1503. She must have felt like she was running out of time to enjoy her eldest girl and also prepare her for the challenges that lay ahead – we know that the two spent a great deal of time together when they were both in the capital, with the little Queen of Scots always walking a few paces behind her mother and sitting at her side at meals or when they were hearing Mass in the royal chapel. On top of all this family stress there were rumours that the royal marriage was in trouble, thanks in part to Elizabeth's peripatetic wanderings and long absences from court over the summer and autumn of 1502, but it's more likely that they were simply giving each other the space to deal with the enormous burden of their grief in different ways – in Elizabeth's case this required a change of scenery, new faces and travel.

Whatever had happened during the summer, the couple were very much together again at Christmas, which was held with all the usual festive pomp and celebration. The new baby wasn't due until early spring and there were plans afoot for Elizabeth to take to a splendidly appointed birthing chamber at Richmond Palace well before she was expected to go into labour. However, she went into labour several weeks early while still residing in the less impressive, but still magnificent, royal apartments of the Tower of London, which at the beginning of the sixteenth century was still one of the Tudor family's favourite residences and not at all the dank prison of later imaginings. Luckily, Elizabeth's usual midwife, Alice Massey, who had delivered all of her previous babies, was on hand to assist as the queen gave birth on 2 February – not to the much hoped for second son, but yet another girl.

The baby, who was named Catherine in honour of the queen's sister and daughter-in-law, was weak and not expected to thrive so she was quickly whisked away to be baptised in the chapel of St Peter ad Vincula church within the Tower precincts without any of the fuss and pageantry that had attended the christenings of her elder siblings. It had been a difficult and painful labour and it's unlikely that anyone was very surprised when Queen Elizabeth failed to recover from her ordeal as quickly as usual. Physicians were sent for, one from as far away as Plymouth in Devon, but the alarm wasn't really raised until a week after the birth, on 9 February, when the ailing queen's condition took a decided turn for the worse and her husband and family truly began to be afraid for her life. King Henry, half mad with worry, spent hours in prayer but it was all in vain – Elizabeth, the wife he had taken as a matter of necessity and then fallen deeply in love with, died two days later on her thirty-seventh birthday with her husband at her side.

The baby that she had sacrificed herself to bring into the world passed away a week later.

Henry was devastated by Elizabeth's death and secluded himself for several weeks in order to privately mourn her. She had been a calming, soothing presence in his often troubled life for almost sixteen years, had won his trust and devotion and borne him several children. For many people, Elizabeth of York was the very epitome of how a queen should be – beautiful, kind, gracious and, outwardly at least, meek and the outpouring of genuine grief, both at home and abroad, that greeted her death only served to prove just how beloved she had been. For her three surviving children, Elizabeth's death was a dreadful blow that would almost certainly haunt them for the rest of their lives. Prince Henry, who had been extremely close to his mother, was particularly affected by his bereavement and it has been suggested that this early loss of the woman he had considered to be the epitome of perfect womanhood led to his later dramatic matrimonial history as he searched for someone who could compare to the idealised memory of his mother.

In the collection of the National Library of Wales there resides the Vaux Passional, a remarkable illuminated manuscript that dates from the period immediately after the death of Elizabeth of York, with a frontispiece that gives a moving glimpse of the aftermath of the terrible events of February 1503. King Henry is depicted in the foreground, crowned and dressed in grey and blue mourning for his wife – albeit accessorised with a lovely pair of crimson hose – while in the background, the artist has painted the three royal children – Mary and Margaret (who faces the viewer and wears a black mourning hood and pink dress) are shown sitting in front of the fire, while the red-headed Prince Henry is a solitary figure at the back, hiding his face as he weeps on his mother's now empty bed. It's an unusually honest and poignant depiction of a grieving family, especially for this period, and is indicative of just how deeply unhappy they all were. None of the royal children were present at Elizabeth's magnificent state funeral, which took place in London at the end of February and concluded with a torchlit ceremony in Westminster Abbey, where Elizabeth's sister Catherine, Countess of Dorset, acted as chief mourner. The children had their opportunity to say goodbye the day after their mother's death, when they were taken in to see her body, washed and dressed in her robes of state, lying on her bed. They would never see her again.

For Margaret it must have been a particularly sad time as she prepared for her rapidly approaching wedding without her mother's comforting presence. Elizabeth had taken a close interest in the arrangements for Margaret's departure, especially in the more fun aspects like ordering her expansive trousseau; shortly before she died, Elizabeth paid for one of Margaret's crimson velvet gowns to be richly trimmed with black pampilion, an expensive fur that closely resembled Persian lamb. From now on, the young princess would have to rely on her grandmother, Lady Margaret Beaufort, for advice as she prepared to leave England, while her father, who left his self imposed seclusion at the end of March, took charge of her trousseau, which was poignantly ordered alongside her mourning clothes for her mother. The royal account ledgers have several entries detailing the beautiful clothes that were being ordered for Margaret's new life as Queen of Scotland – black satin and velvet, cloth of gold, purple velvet, tawny damask and crimson satin gowns with detachable crimson, gold, green, black and tawny satin and sarcenet sleeves, fur trimmings and lace and ribbon embellishments. Margaret's trousseau also included fine linen chemises, stockings, two dozen pairs of gloves, three yards of black velvet for hoods and other accessories, crimson and scarlet hats, six pairs of shoes, ermine night bonnets, an opulent black velvet nightgown and a veritable mountain of the pins and ribbons considered necessary to hold Tudor fashions together. No expense was spared in order to ensure that Margaret dazzled her new Scottish subjects with her elegance and refinement.

The royal craftsmen were also being kept busy producing opulent new furnishings for Margaret to take with her to Scotland, including a chair of state, cloth-of-gold hung litter, canopy and crimson sarcenet hangings lavishly embroidered with Tudor red roses for her state bed, which was also provided with cloth-of-gold and yellow damask trimmings, gold fringing and a green velvet counterpane as well as fine-linen bedding. Her entourage was equally splendidly equipped – the royal accounts include lists of clothes that were ordered for her ladies and gentlemen and her father also ordered livery for the two footmen and other servants that would be accompanying her up north. Her male servants were provided with two sets of livery which comprised a pair of black velvet doublets embroidered with the Tudor portcullis badge to be worn with either a green and white cloth-of-gold jacket or a plainer green damask jacket.

Margaret's departure was scheduled for June and it must have been an exciting time for her, despite all of the sorrow about her mother's death. Lady Catherine Gordon, the widow of the pretender Perkin Warbeck, was to accompany her to Scotland and she would no doubt have spent a great deal of time telling the young princess all about the Scottish court and the man who presided over it. However, it is very unlikely that Lady Catherine made any mention of King James's various notorious affairs with the ladies of that court, in particular his two favourite long term mistresses Marion Boyd and Janet Kennedy, the latter of whom had given birth to three of his children and openly resided in splendid apartments in Stirling Castle, which was now to be part of Margaret Tudor's jointure. It is even less likely that she made any mention of the beautiful Margaret Drummond, who had briefly been his mistress and given birth to James's daughter in the late 1490s before dying in suspicious circumstances in 1501 along with her two sisters, Euphemia and Sibylla. It's likely that the three Drummond sisters died of food poisoning, but of course it didn't take long for rumours to flourish that Margaret had been deliberately targeted and poisoned by English secret agents because she was perceived to be a threat to her lover's match with Margaret Tudor, which had not at that stage been finalised.

There was even a spurious story, supported by the inscription over Margaret Drummond's tomb in front of the altar of Dunblane Cathedral, that the royal mistress had actually been secretly married to King James and had therefore been liquidated by a group of Scottish nobles who were determined not to let this detail get in the way of his union with the English princess. It has also, rather preposterously, been suggested that Lady Margaret Beaufort had a hand in the plot – after all the terrible trouble that rumours of Edward IV's secret marriage to Eleanor Butler had caused for Elizabeth of York and her family, it was likely that even the merest hint of a morganatic match on the part of a prospective Tudor suitor would be likely to bring negotiations to a swift and decisive end. This is all conjecture though – James IV was no fool and would be very unlikely to imperil this all-important chance to raise his country's prestige by making a clandestine marriage with someone else. Nonetheless, it's certain that no stories about her future husband's romantic escapades were likely to have reached Margaret's ears as she quietly prepared to join him in Scotland.

Chapter 6

Farewells 1503

The years of diplomatic negotiation and then months of feverish preparation came to an end on 27 June 1503 when Margaret finally left Richmond Palace for her new life. Unexpectedly, her father decided to accompany her for the first stage of her epic journey, which would take her to the most northern reaches of his kingdom before she crossed the border into Scotland. Henry had been left depressed and prematurely aged by the loss of his wife just five months earlier and doubtless didn't feel quite ready to let his eldest daughter go too, even under happier circumstances and, although she would still be inhabiting the same relatively small island, there were no guarantees that they would ever get the opportunity to see each other again. Margaret's first stop on her journey was Collyweston Palace near Stamford in Northamptonshire, the main country residence of her grandmother Lady Margaret Beaufort. The royal party stayed at Collyweston for eleven days, which was spent making the final preparations for the main journey while also enjoying the lavish round of entertainments that Margaret Beaufort had laid on for her guests.

It was a beautiful, balmy summer and the young people of the party no doubt spent much of their time outdoors enjoying the extensive gardens with the new terraces and ponds that their hostess had recently installed, probably in anticipation of their visit. At the end of the visit, Lady Margaret hosted an intimate farewell party for her granddaughter, where the only guests were blood relatives of the Tudor clan, who gathered together in order to say goodbye. However, the most painful goodbyes, with her father, siblings, aunts and grandmother, took place in private, away from the gaze of the numerous servants and courtiers that surrounded the Tudor royal family at all times. Although everyone hoped that she would be able to visit at some point in the future, they all knew that such an event was extremely unlikely to ever come to pass and that they were, in all probability, saying goodbye for the very last time. Henry, an always self-contained and quiet man who had emerged from his seclusion after Elizabeth's death even more reserved than ever, seems to have been particularly affected by the parting, which no doubt came upon them all far too quickly. Before Margaret left Collyweston, he presented her with an exquisite illuminated Book of Hours from 'your kind and loving father', and made her promise to pray for him and write as often as possible.

Margaret parted from her father and grandmother for the last time on 8 July, before leaving on the next leg of her long journey to Scotland, which was expected to take just over a month and would involve long hours in the saddle punctuated with a gruelling schedule of official receptions at every town and city she passed through with her vast entourage. Her father entrusted her to the care of Thomas Howard, Earl of Surrey, and his domineering wife Agnes Tilney, who would act as her chaperones until she had been safely delivered to Scotland. Margaret was not overly fond of the Earl and Countess of Surrey but was nonetheless forced to endure their company and follow their direction for the next few weeks, no doubt fully aware that any rebellion, no matter how satisfyingly petty, would be immediately reported back to her father and grandmother. Thomas Howard had only recently been returned to royal favour after fighting for Richard III at Bosworth, where his father had been killed, which had resulted in his being summarily stripped of his title and lands and imprisoned in the Tower of London for the next three years. By 1503 however, his title and much of his lands had been restored, he had a seat on the Council and had been appointed Lord High Chancellor. This temporary guardianship of Margaret was yet another sign that the Howard family were once again firmly ensconced in the royal good books and from this point on, no other aristocratic family would be quite so closely linked to the fortunes and, more specifically, the chequered romantic history of the Tudor dynasty. For Surrey, a military man who was more used to directing troops than acting as duenna to a wilful adolescent girl, the next few weeks would be a huge strain as he orchestrated every detail of Margaret's journey while at the same time did his best to ensure that she was as comfortable as possible.

However, if Surrey found the trip stressful, it was doubly so for his strong willed young charge. Margaret was just 13-years-old, small for her age, petulant and extremely fond of getting her own way – it did not please her to dance to someone else's tune and although she usually enjoyed being the centre of attention, she was often bored and irritated by the constant round of entertainments and official functions that marked each stop on her journey. She spent long hours in the saddle every day and although everyone in her entourage did their best to ensure her comfort at all times, it must have been a deeply uncomfortable, wearisome and annoying experience all the same. Her father and grandmother had planned every detail of her journey and carefully picked the noble families who would be hosting her in their homes along the way – they were all faithful supporters of the Tudor family, who could be relied upon to take special care of their honoured guest and her entourage, who would arrive exhausted, saddle- sore and weary after a day of riding, and then have to face an evening of banqueting and entertainments that might go on until late at night.

King Henry was gratified to receive reports of his daughter's enthusiastic reception as she travelled further north because it confirmed how popular and respected the Tudor clan were in England, but for his daughter, who had never before been so far away from home and was now suddenly thrust into the role of unofficial ambassadress for the family, it was very hard work indeed. Although she was not without her own charm, Margaret lacked the enormous charisma and all important common touch that her siblings, especially Henry, had inherited from their famously handsome and gregarious Plantagenet grandfather Edward IV and so she struggled to inspire loyalty in her entourage or to excite much admiration in those who beheld her during her slow progress north. That she was pretty, knew how to behave in public and, thanks to the enormous sums spent on her trousseau, looked every inch the princess could not be disputed, but she clearly lacked the certain 'something' that would make men flock to her younger sister Mary, and made her brother Henry the cynosure of all eyes whenever he appeared in public.

Thanks to the Somerset herald, John Young, who had been ordered to accompany her to Scotland and write a detailed report of the events of her journey, presumably for the benefit of her absent father and grandmother, we have vivid descriptions of the young Queen of Scots magnificently dressed in velvet, cloth-of-gold and fur, bedecked in jewels, mounted on a white palfrey and surrounded by her equally elegantly dressed ladies-in-waiting. He describes how the church bells pealed and the excited populace, who were no doubt considerably enlivened by large quantities of free ale, cheered and threw their caps in the air as the vast procession rode by, with some of the gentlemen tossing gold coins into the crowd as they went. Margaret's procession quickly swelled to vast numbers thanks to the tagging along of hundreds of extra people, mostly local landed gentry keen to see a bit of the world and enjoy some rare close proximity to royalty – most of them would leave after a couple of stages but a handful remained with the procession until they reached Scotland, which must have been quite the adventure for those who had never before left home. This ragtag group was expected to follow the strict rules that dictated the order of the procession, which had the Earl of Surrey at its head with his soldiers, followed by the gentlemen in order of precedence, with Surrey's son-in-law – the then relatively obscure Thomas Boleyn – among their ranks, and then Margaret herself, who was preceded by her standard bearer Sir Davy Owen and followed by her Master of the Horse Sir Thomas Wortley, who led her spare palfrey behind him.

Her younger ladies-in-waiting and their squires rode behind on their own horses, while the four older ladies, which probably included the Countess of Surrey, travelled in a magnificent carriage pulled by a team of six horses. Behind the principal ladies-in-waiting rode the less important ladies of Margaret's household, followed by the squires, pageboys and less important gentlemen, all of whom wore the distinctive Tudor livery. There was also a large troupe of musicians, who entertained Margaret and her companions during the long, tedious hours of the journey and also, in the case of the drummers and trumpeters, loudly announced her arrival whenever she was about to enter a town or village along the way. Margaret's baggage carts, which contained the expensive clothes and furnishings that had been provided for her new life as Queen of Scotland as well as her personal belongings, went on ahead to their next stop with her personal retinue of kitchen staff and servants, so that everything could be prepared for her arrival. Each wagon was covered with green and white canvas, the Tudor colours, and bedecked with the arms and symbols of England and Scotland as well as the ubiquitous Lancastrian red roses.

The first stop after leaving Collyweston was nearby Grantham, where Margaret was greeted by the Sheriff of Lincoln, Sir Robert Dymock before resting for the night at Hall Place (now known as Grantham House) as the guest of the wealthy mercantile Hall family. After this she rode on to Newark-on-Trent, where she stayed in the castle and was richly entertained by the local nobility. Also on her route was Tuxford, the Carmelite Whitefriars friary in Doncaster, where she prayed before the shrine of Our Lady of Doncaster, Pontefract Castle and Tadcaster in North Yorkshire, where she was joined by Lord and Lady Latimer, the future parents-in-law of her brother's sixth wife Catherine Parr.

Another new arrival was the 5th Earl of Northumberland, one of her father's favourite courtiers, possibly due to the fact that King Henry had once been betrothed to his mother, Maude Herbert, sister of the Earl of Pembroke. Like Surrey, Northumberland came from a family with a chequered past – his father had been one of Richard III's closest friends and supporters and had been entrusted with the Yorkist reserve troops at Bosworth – which spectacularly backfired for Richard when Northumberland refused to send them into the battle, which was a significant factor in Henry Tudor's victory. The 26-year-old earl had recently been appointed Warden of the Eastern March, which made him responsible for the security and governance of the eastern section of the English side of the border between England and Scotland while his opposite number on the Scottish side was Patrick Hepburn, Earl of Bothwell, who had acted as King James's proxy at the betrothal ceremony. Like a lot of other extremely wealthy and handsome young men, Northumberland loved to live well and spent a great deal of money on clothes and personal embellishment, which probably didn't endear him to the warrior Earl of Surrey, but made him a great favourite of Margaret and her ladies, who also greatly appreciated his displays of horsemanship. John Young, the Somerset herald, seems to have been equally dazzled by the Earl of Northumberland and made a point of describing his clothes in his chronicle, starting with the crimson velvet mantle, splendid jewels and black velvet boots, which he wore when he first met up with the cavalcade on the way to York.

The great northern city of York was in the very heartland of the old Yorkist territory and had remained loyal to her father's rival Richard III to the bitter end, although it had swiftly pledged its loyalty to King Henry in the wake of Bosworth and had fulsomely welcomed him when he visited a year after his accession. Some of the old loyalties and rivalries still lingered though and although, as daughter of the much loved and respected Yorkist heiress Queen Elizabeth, Margaret had no reason to fear even the most diehard of the remaining Yorkist supporters, even so the mood was undoubtedly tense as her entourage neared the outskirts of the city. Keen to make a good impression, Margaret changed into a new cloth-of-gold gown and swapped her horse for a cloth-of-gold litter before continuing on to the city's imposing turreted Micklegate Bar entrance, which was traditionally used by members of the royal family when they visited from the south.

Less pleasantly, the severed heads of Margaret's great grandfather, Richard, Duke of York, and his 17-year-old son Edmund of Rutland had been displayed on Micklegate by the victorious Lancastrian army after the battle of Wakefield in 1460 and it is to be hoped that no one informed Margaret of this as she entered the city. By the time her entourage reached York on 15 July it had swelled to such enormous proportions that the Mayor, Sir John Guillot panicked and ordered that a large hole should be created in the city walls to allow the procession to enter unimpeded. Once they entered the city, Margaret and her retinue were greeted by astonishing scenes as the vast crowds gathered to see her erupted into spontaneous cheers and rushed forward to get a closer look. It took over two hours for the procession to reach York Minster, where the Archbishop of York, Thomas Savage, a cousin of Lady Margaret Beaufort's husband Lord Stanley, was waiting to greet her, surrounded by a gaggle of Bishops. Margaret was then escorted to the Archbishop's Palace behind the Minster, where she was to lodge for the next two nights.

The following morning, Margaret was up early to hear Mass in the minster, yet again dressing with special care for the occasion in another cloth-of-gold gown, which she wore with a bejewelled collar and exquisitely wrought gold girdle that hung to her feet. Lady Surrey carried the young queen's train as she progressed up the aisle to the place of honour immediately before the pulpit, past all the great and good of York and the surrounding area who had crammed into the minster to catch a glimpse of her. After Mass, Margaret returned on foot to the Archbishop's palace where Northumberland, who was also dressed to impress in cloth-of-gold encrusted with precious stones, presented his wife, Catherine Spencer, whose mother, Eleanor Beaufort, was a cousin of Margaret's grandmother, Lady Margaret Beaufort. After this there was a banquet and another evening of splendid entertainments for Margaret's benefit. Before she left York the following day, 17 July, the city's officials presented her with a gilt bowl filled to the rim with gold coins, which was added to the growing stash of rich wedding gifts that she accumulated during her progress north.

The next major stop on her journey, after minor stays at Newburgh Priory, Northallerton and Darlington, was the cathedral city of Durham, where she attended Mass in the cathedral and spent three days in the castle as the guest of the newly inaugurated Bishop of Durham, Richard Foxe, who spared no expense and threw a huge public banquet in her honour on 23 July. After Durham, Margaret moved on to Newcastle, where she was greeted at the city gates by a crowd of children singing hymns before she made her state entry, riding past the quayside, where the more intrepid spectators climbed the masts of the docked ships in order to get a closer look at their king's eldest daughter. Newcastle put on a good show for Margaret, but John Young disapprovingly noted in his record of the event that unlike the other cities, they did not honour the Queen of Scots with a gun salute, adding that this oversight might have been due to a lack of powder.

In Newcastle, Margaret stayed not in the castle, which dominated the city, but in Austin Friars, the home of the Augustinian monks, where, as always, she was well looked after with the best chambers, entertainments and food. The following day was 25 July, the Feast of St James the Apostle, which was considered a highly propitious occasion for a girl who was on her way to marry King James of Scotland. Accordingly, she heard Mass in Newcastle Cathedral in the morning and later on attended an extravagant banquet hosted by the Earl of Northumberland in his mansion, which went on until midnight and was, by all accounts, a magnificent affair involving plenty of 'dances, sports and songs'. One of the most honoured guests was the formidable warrior lord and Warden of the Western March Thomas Dacre, 2nd Baron Dacre of Gilsland, who had been appointed Lord Warden of the Marches in 1495 and was one of the most powerful men in the north.

Like Surrey and Northumberland's father, Dacre had been a loyal Yorkist and had fought on the side of Richard III at Bosworth before pledging his loyalty to the victorious King Henry immediately after the battle and, like the others, remaining in the royal good books ever since, to the extent that he was entrusted with important offices in the kingdom, including ones that pertained to the realm's defence against Scotland. The following day, the no doubt weary Margaret left Newcastle and travelled on to Morpeth in Northumberland, where she was escorted by the Sheriff to Newminster Abbey, home to the Cistercian order, where she heard a service in the chapel before retiring to her chambers. After leaving Morpeth she rode on to Alnwick Castle, the imposing seat of the Earl of Northumberland, where she stayed for two days and was most royally entertained. On one of the days, the company went hunting and Margaret impressed everyone by shooting down a fine buck with her bow and arrow.

After leaving Alnwick, Margaret rode on to Berwick-upon-Tweed, which was to be her last stop on the English side of the border, just two and a half miles away to the north. Berwick was a fortified stronghold that had been hotly contested by both the English and Scottish for centuries, swapping hands several times along the way. By 1503 it was firmly controlled by the English, and the subject of its own protective clause in Margaret's marriage treaty; the arrival of the king's daughter was the excuse for much celebration and fanfare – including a hearty gun salute, which delighted John Young. Margaret remained in Berwick for two days and enjoyed the usual round of entertainments as well as a day of hunting and, less pleasantly, bear baiting.

Despite all the fun and frivolity on offer, it must have been a strange and emotional time for Margaret, who was now within days of crossing the border to Scotland, leaving behind her old, familiar, comfortable existence as the eldest English princess and beginning her new life as a wife and a queen. She was just 13-years-old and had been on the road for exactly a month since leaving Richmond Palace. Although she was surrounded by familiar faces, in some cases people she had known all her life, she was no doubt missing her family, homesick for the life she had left behind, weary of being on show for hours on end and completely fed up with moving from place to place. On the other hand, her progress north through her father's realm had provided her with a unique glimpse of the most northern parts of the kingdom as even King Henry had never made it any further than York. This was also a rare opportunity for the people of the north to set eyes on a member of the royal family, and clearly they relished the chance to get as close as possible to Margaret whenever she made one of her frequent stops along the way.

Her father's predecessor, Richard III, had been much loved in the north of the country and had spent a lot of time there over the years, which made him a hard act to follow. It was for this reason that King Henry had made a point of visiting the north in the first year of his reign, taking his wife Elizabeth with him but they had not since returned, which made Margaret the first official royal visitor for over a decade. She must have been delighted and also alarmed by the ecstatic welcome that she received. The fact that her marriage was regarded as the harbinger of peace between Scotland and England and an end to the hostilities that had ravaged the borders for centuries only added to her appeal and made the celebrations all the more fervent. It was to be the last royal progress of the north for almost forty years, until Margaret's younger brother Henry VIII, escorted by his fifth wife Catherine Howard, travelled to York in 1541 in order to have an ultimately abortive meeting with James V.

By 1541, much of the north experienced by Margaret had vanished thanks to her brother's Reformation and the dissolution of the monasteries and religious buildings. Most of the beautiful old monasteries and abbeys she stayed in during her progress were closed down, their inhabitants forcibly defrocked and the lands either sold on or given away to favoured courtiers. Stately Newminster Abbey in Morpeth, where she stayed as the guest of the Cistercian monks, was dissolved in 1537 and quickly fell into a state of disrepair after being leased to the Grey family who plundered the stone for their other building projects, while the Austin Friars where she stayed during her visit to Newcastle was closed down in 1540 and later fell into the hands of John Dudley, 1st Duke of Northumberland.

Margaret left Berwick-on-Tweed on the first day of August 1503, escorted by an entourage that had by now swelled to accommodate over

2,000 people. Once she had crossed the border into Scotland, Margaret rode to Lamberton, a small estate three miles north of Berwick, where she was scheduled to be formally welcomed to her new kingdom by the Archbishop of Glasgow, the Bishop of Moray and the several hundred Scottish gentlemen who had accompanied them. The Archbishop, Robert Blackadder, was obviously already familiar to Margaret as he had performed her proxy marriage ceremony in Richmond Palace and she was no doubt very pleased to see him again at the end of her long and exhausting journey. Once the formal welcoming ceremony was over, Margaret was escorted to a large pavilion that had been erected nearby, where some of the ladies of the Scottish court were waiting to be introduced to her and present gifts of fresh fruit. After this, Margaret said a regretful farewell to the dashing Earl of Northumberland and most of her makeshift entourage, whose adventure was now at an end.

Not everyone left her though – the Surreys would remain with Margaret until she was safely married and a further 500 members of her English escort also opted to stay until the wedding had taken place. They now followed her to Fast Castle, a forbidding coastal fortress overlooking the North Sea, where she was to spend her first night on Scottish soil. Although her hosts Lord and Lady Home obviously made sure that Margaret had the best of everything and that her stay was a comfortable one, she must have felt apprehensive as she passed beneath the drawbridge then rode across the bridge over a ravine to the main keep, which had been built on a bleak rock plateau that towered 45 metres above the sea. Luckily, Margaret spent just one night at Fast Castle before continuing her progress, this time on the Scottish side of the border.

The first stop was Haddington in East Lothian, where she spent the night in a local abbey before riding to lovely Dalkeith Castle on the banks of the river Esk, home of John Douglas, 2nd Earl of Morton and his Countess, Janet Crichton on 3 August. The earl's mother was Princess Joan of Scotland, a daughter of James I and his English wife Joan Beaufort, which made him a relative of both King James and, more distantly, Margaret through her grandmother. The Mortons were consequently extremely powerful, although they mostly eschewed court life in favour of enjoying their estates. The earl greeted Margaret warmly just outside the castle, while his countess, who was waiting at the castle gates, dropped to her knees before their new queen, who immediately raised her up and kissed her as a mark of great favour. As they were both tremendously wealthy and eager to please, the Mortons put on a lavish display for their honoured guest – but nothing they had organised for Margaret's entertainment could compete with the excited anticipation of their other special guest who was also scheduled to arrive at the castle later in the day. In this age of proxy weddings, arranged marriages and dynastic alliances, it had become the custom to at least pretend that there was still a romantic, spontaneous element to the marriages of the great and good, in part to reflect the hopes of everyone involved that the marriage would be a happy one with true love eventually blossoming between the couple and a happy ending for all concerned.

By the early sixteenth century, it had become customary for a bridegroom to pre-empt the formal meeting with his bride with an 'accidental' rendezvous in a more informal setting. Not only was this more pleasant for everyone, it was also intended as a compliment to the bride because it suggested that her future husband was so impatient to behold her beauty that he risked breaking the rules of etiquette, which generally contrived to keep betrothed couples apart before they were married. In some cases, the suitor and his companions turned up in disguise, which added to the fun and made it more like a real life masque or mummery. In the case of Margaret's elder brother, Prince Arthur, this charade went very well indeed when he and his father surprised the evidently charmed and delighted Catherine of Aragon but it did not go so well for her younger brother Henry when he dropped in on his fourth bride Anne of Cleves, who did not recognise him and reacted with maidenly horror and disgust to his advances. Naturally everyone hoped that James and Margaret's first meeting would go as well as that of Prince Arthur and the Spanish Infanta and finally, after all the years of negotiation and anticipation, they were about to find out what the couple thought of each other in the flesh.

Chapter 7

Meetings 1503

Although he was not, as a rule, adverse to a bit of dressing up, James evidently decided against it on this occasion and instead claimed to be conveniently enjoying a hunting party in a nearby forest when news arrived of his bride's arrival, upon which he naturally hastened to meet her. Accompanied by his younger brother, the Earl of Ross, as well as the Earls of Lennox, Argyll and Huntly and a large company of his favourite courtiers, he arrived shortly after Margaret, dressed for hunting in a richly embroidered crimson velvet jacket but with his beloved lyre slung over his shoulders in order to proclaim that he had come to woo, not to kill. He hurried up the stairs and met Margaret, who had been warned in advance of his attentions and taken the opportunity to freshen up and change into one of her best dresses, at the entrance to her apartments.

While everyone else politely pretended to look elsewhere, the couple exchanged reverences, no doubt looking each other over as they did so, then chastely kissed before Margaret led James into her chamber to meet her ladies, each of whom also received a polite welcoming kiss from the Scottish king. She then introduced him to the Earl of Surrey and the other high ranking English noblemen who had escorted her to Dalkeith, after which the couple sat down together to talk, covertly watched by the rest of the room. Luckily for Margaret, James was a charming and witty conversationalist and so would have known exactly how to put her at her ease and make her laugh. He continued to amuse her at dinner, where they were seated together and enjoyed the entertainments that had been thoughtfully provided by their hosts. After dinner, encouraged by James, Margaret danced for the company with the Countess of Surrey as her partner – she may not have been the most academically gifted of the Tudor children but the dance floor, along with the hunting field, was somewhere that she did excel and so she was very keen to show off the fruits of all those long hours spent learning dance steps with her tutors.

When the evening came to an end, James took an affectionate but respectful leave of his young bride and rode back to Edinburgh with his companions, apparently very well pleased with how their first meeting had gone. Although he had received a portrait of Margaret while negotiating for her hand in marriage, James would still have been anxious to see her with his own eyes. Not that it mattered much anyway – it was far too late to back out of the marriage, even if he had found her completely repulsive. As for Margaret, it's fair to assume that she too was very happy with the match that had been arranged for her. James had only just turned 30 and was good looking, energetic, healthy, charismatic and clearly in the prime of his life. He was very attractive to women and he adored them in return, treating both his aristocratic official mistresses and more casual encounters, many of whom came from the lower classes, with the same polite courtesy and respect. He was also the very pattern of a courteous Renaissance prince when it came to his treatment of his illegitimate children – all of whom he recognised as his own and lavished with every possible advantage. Margaret would be less than pleased when she discovered that her charming new husband had other claims upon his affection, but she was still unable to fault the level of attention, care and consideration that he managed to show her at all times. If he had been able to follow his own inclination, then it's possible that James would have married his favourite mistress Janet Kennedy, who was mother to three of his illegitimate children, but this was never an option, not least because she may have already been married. However, even if James was not able to marry the woman he truly loved, then he was at least very well pleased with the bride that circumstances, and a pressing need to ally himself with his English neighbours, had given him.

Fresh from her first exciting and successful meeting with her husband, Margaret was doubtless in an extremely good mood when she went to bed in her chambers at Dalkeith Castle that night, but the following morning brought the bad news that the castle's stables had gone up in flames during the night and that several of her horses had perished in the fire along with much of her splendid riding gear, including a new cloth-of-gold caparison (the cloth that covered a horse beneath the saddle). Like all the Tudors, Margaret was passionately fond of horses, and she was initially inconsolable about their loss. However, by the time James, who had hastened to see her as soon as the news of the fire got to Edinburgh, arrived in Dalkeith, she had recovered her composure enough to be merrily playing cards when he entered her rooms.

The rest of the day passed as pleasantly as the previous evening had done, with more music and dancing, the latter led by Margaret and Viscount Lisle, the son-in-law of the Earl of Surrey. Later on, James himself entertained the company by playing the clavichord and his lute with remarkable skill and then singing a duet with one of the Scottish gentlemen that he had brought with him. When he left later in the evening, he impressed everyone, and especially his bride to be, by jumping straight into his horse's saddle without using the stirrups. He was back again the next evening and this time it was Margaret's turn to show off the musical skills she had been taught at her father's court by playing the clavichord and then her own lute, almost certainly the one her mother had paid to have re-stringed just before her death, while James sat on the floor beside her in a lover like pose. James won further praise from the English later on when he offered Margaret his place of honour at the supper table after she complained about her own chair being too uncomfortable.

Their halcyon wooing at Dalkeith Castle came to an end on 7 August when Margaret, richly dressed in cloth-of-gold, trimmed with black velvet and a dazzling necklace of pearls and precious stones, climbed into her gold bedecked litter to make her much anticipated journey to the Scottish capital Edinburgh. Behind her trotted an elegant palfrey with a sumptuous caparison made from five ells of gold cloth – one of the horses that James had given her to replace those lost in the stable fire and a lovely white hart, a traditional lover's gift that had also been presented to Margaret by the Scottish king.

Margaret's entourage was met half way by James, also dressed in cloth-of-gold with black fur trimmings, who dismounted in order to kiss his bride before jumping back into the saddle and riding alongside her litter for the rest of the journey. It was a lovely summer's day and there was a lighthearted carnival atmosphere as the procession rode through the beautiful Scottish countryside. Everyone was dressed in cloth-of-gold, rich velvets and shimmering silks, while their horses were equally lavishly decorated with freshly polished bridles and embroidered caparisons beneath their saddles. They were accompanied by musicians and the air was filled with music, singing and laughter as they jauntily rode towards the capital with James and Margaret at their head, proceeded by a gentleman bearing the sheathed sword of state with its purple velvet scabbard which had the words 'In my Defens God me Defende', the motto of the royal house of Scotland, picked out in pearls.

Just outside the city, they encountered two young knights, Sir Patrick Hamilton and Patrick Sinclair, enthusiastically performing a mock duel for the honour of an absent lady, which quickly turned out to be an allegorical illusion to the triumphs and tribulations of courtly romance. After James had laughingly brought the fighting to a halt, Margaret's new white hart was released into the meadow, where it was chased by one of James's greyhounds – however, luckily for the hart, this too turned out to be an allegory as it was speedily rescued. Once all the excitement was over, Margaret was invited to descend from her litter and helped up on to the back of James's horse so that she was sharing his saddle. Luckily for her, the king's original plan to carry her into the capital on the back of his favourite war horse was overturned when James and one of his gentlemen tested it and realised that the plan would inevitably lead to disaster and so instead Margaret's own more sweet-natured new palfrey was hastily substituted. Still, it must have been a strange sensation for Margaret, who had been raised in the sheltered environment of the Tudor royal nursery, to suddenly find herself in such close proximity to a man who was not a blood relation, and indeed forced to clasp her arms tightly around his waist to stop herself falling.

This sharing of a horse was not normal procedure at the time and nor was it considered usual for a reigning monarch to share his bride's state entry to her new capital. That James chose to do so was just another part of the sweet little romantic pantomime he had been performing since Margaret's arrival, in which he had cast himself as her ardent and devoted suitor while she was his one and only love to be both wooed and protected. There was no need, of course, for James to go to these lengths to obscure the unsentimental, political reasons for their marriage and instead reframe it as a love match, but nonetheless this is what he set out to do. In the process he mollified the English noblemen who had accompanied Margaret over the border into Scotland and also, more importantly, allayed any fears that his bride, who was still four months short of her fourteenth birthday, must have had about him.

All those long hours spent talking to Margaret, flattering her and making her laugh, then sitting at her feet as she played her lute, were designed to both set his bride at ease while at the same time setting the tone for their future relationship, which he obviously hoped would be warm, affectionate and mutually respectful. However, despite all of the romantic overtones, the fact still remained that Scotland was very much England's inferior both in size and also prestige, and in casting himself as the lovelorn, devoted suitor in this royal romance, James was acknowledging this fact. There was also something primitive and possessive about the way he insisted upon carrying Margaret into Edinburgh behind him on his horse, as if she was his captive or a hostage rather than the honoured princess of a rival royal house.

By rights, Margaret should have been paraded through the streets of her new capital in her costly cloth-of-gold litter, with the curtains pulled back so that the people could see her as she went past, but instead the trappings of royalty were stripped from her and she was carried back like a trophy from a foreign war – which in some ways is exactly what she was. To the teenage princess, this treatment probably seemed bold, exciting and completely unlike anything she had ever experienced, whereas to her husband it was all part of a much larger, more sophisticated game with the ultimate goal of increasing Scotland's power on the world stage.

The couple were greeted with cheers as they halted at the city gates, where a young woman dressed as an angel presented Margaret with the key to the city. This was just the first of a series of staged tableaux that greeted the royal couple's procession down the Royal Mile to Holyrood Palace, all of which were designed to celebrate their union, the grandeur of their respective royal houses and the beauty of the new Queen of Scots. One elaborate tableau involved a fanciful interpretation of the Judgement of Paris, while another involved a re-enactment of the annunciation with the Virgin Mary kneeling before the angel Gabriel. Wine flowed from a fountain by St Giles Church on the Royal Mile and Margaret would have seen intertwined thistles and red roses, the symbols of Scotland and the Tudor royal house, everywhere she looked. It was her first ever glimpse of the Scottish capital and like several other first time visitors from England and further afield, she was probably surprised and impressed by the attractiveness and geniality of the populace, who were often characterised as ill-favoured and surly, if not downright villainous, by their English neighbours. The city centre was relatively well appointed and pleasant, especially in the area immediately around the Royal Mile – although it was much less salubrious further out, especially close to the docks at Leith.

In 1503, Edinburgh had a population of around 12,000 people, which made it significantly smaller than London, which was home to over 80,000, and not much larger than York, England's second largest city, which had a population of around 10,000. Having been raised in the sheltered, privileged environment of the Tudor royal palaces, Margaret would have had scant experience of the teeming, noisy streets of central London but even so, she may have found Edinburgh – busy and flourishing though it was – disappointingly small in comparison to her father's capital city. There was still much to admire about the Scottish capital however, and as they slowly rode down the Royal Mile towards Holyrood Palace, James probably pointed out all of the most notable buildings to her, including residences of his courtiers, St Giles Church with its distinctive crown shaped spire, the entrances to winding alleyways known as 'closes' and the Mercat Cross, where royal proclamations were read out to the populace.

Although Edinburgh was dominated by the brooding bulk of its castle, perched on its centuries old hunk of volcanic rock, James had opted instead to turn away from the traditional home of the monarchs of Scotland, which was cramped, windy and unwelcoming, and instead take his young bride to the far more congenial Holyrood Palace at the bottom of the Royal Mile. He was in the process of building a more modern and comfortable palace to replace the apartments in the adjacent abbey's guesthouse, which had previously been used as a makeshift royal residence. Holyrood had been a favourite of the Scottish kings for generations and James was particularly fond of it, even occasionally spending the court Christmas in the guesthouse, drawn by its cosiness and lovely gardens, neither of which were a feature of the far less hospitable Edinburgh Castle. Work had begun in 1501 in anticipation of Margaret's arrival, with James obviously keen to compete with the luxuries of the Tudor royal palaces. Although he had never visited France, he was interested in French art and architecture and so encouraged his architects to introduce a distinctly French flavour to the new royal palace, which stood alongside the venerable old abbey built by his ancestor David I in the twelfth century.

James's new palace was built around a quadrangle, with the main reception rooms, including a great hall, long gallery and beautiful chapel on the ground floor, his apartments on the first floor of the north side and communicating with them on the south, Margaret's splendidly decorated new rooms, which overlooked the gardens. As was customary, Margaret's rooms mirrored her husband's and incorporated a great chamber underpinned by imported Baltic wood. The window panes were decorated with the intertwined thistle and rose of Scotland and England, and beautiful tapestries covered the walls. It was followed by an equally well-appointed inner chamber, which was a more intimate affair, where Margaret could entertain guests and foreign dignitaries. At the heart of her apartments was a lavishly decorated bedchamber, dominated by her cloth-of-gold bed of state, and with red and purple-blue hangings which had cost her husband £369 to procure. There was also a closet, which housed her close stool (a relatively new innovation in Scotland) and her wardrobe, which housed her enormous collection of clothes and jewels, which now included the pieces that had belonged to her husband's mother, Margaret of Denmark. No expense was spared in the effort to impress Margaret and her entourage, with James happily spending the equivalent of £750,000 on his new palace and even more on the wedding celebrations, which would last for several days and involve entertaining several hundred people.

When they finally arrived at Holyrood, they were greeted by James's younger brother, the Duke of Ross, as well as a welcoming committee that comprised every single Scottish bishop and a significant number of the nobility. After dismounting, James put his arm around Margaret's waist, another unusually intimate gesture, and led her inside the abbey, where they were to hear Mass together to give thanks for her safe arrival in Scotland. The sharp-eyed Somerset herald John Young observed that James kept his arm around Margaret for most of the ceremony, refused to kneel unless she did so before him and even waived his right to be first to kiss the holy relics presented to them, indicating that Margaret should take precedence instead. Although some of those present must have found the Scottish king's insistence upon displaying affection towards his young bride somewhat disconcerting, his good manners could not be faulted and it was doubtless agreed that the young Tudor princess was a lucky girl – certainly, other princesses sent so far away from home in order to marry men they had never set eyes upon fared much worse.

What Margaret herself thought of James's behaviour is not known, but it is tempting to speculate that she was in all likelihood reassured by his kindness and consideration. After Mass, the Bishop of Moray introduced Margaret to several of the most prominent ladies of the Scottish court, with her husband's mistresses being notable exceptions, in her great chamber before the couple enjoyed a celebratory feast in the new great hall, which was followed by the usual entertainments, music and dancing. Margaret spent the night alone in her new bedchamber before being woken up early the next morning in order to prepare for her wedding. Although she and James had been bound together by the proxy ceremony in Richmond Palace, it was still necessary for them to be officially married in person. Although Margaret had brought with her a magnificent trousseau of gowns and accessories, her wedding dress was made in Scotland and paid for by her new husband, who intended for them to wear matching outfits for the ceremony. James's accounts reveal that he paid the princely sum of £183 2s 6d for the royal wedding clothes, which were fashioned from a bolt of white damask silk figured with gold thread, then lined with taffeta and crimson velvet. Later, both outfits would be given away – James's to the English heralds, while Margaret's went to the Scottish Officers of Arms – although it would later be bought back and returned to her.

Margaret teamed her gorgeous white and gold damask wedding dress with a gold coronet made by Edinburgh goldsmith John Currour, while her red hair hung loose down her back beneath a richly decorated long gauzy veil, which fell to the floor behind her. The elaborate pearl and precious stone necklace that she had worn on a number of occasions during her journey to Scotland gleamed around her throat. When she left her rooms in the morning, she was escorted by Thomas Savage, the Archbishop of York and the splendidly dressed Earl of Surrey, whose wife, the countess, was in charge of Margaret's heavy ermine lined train, which turned out to be such an onerous task that she was forced to recruit a hapless usher to help. Behind them walked Margaret's English ladies-in-waiting, each of whom was escorted by a Scottish lady of equal rank in a pleasing display of unity between the two nations that was also intended to delicately prevent any fallings-out over rank and precedence.

The bridal party went on foot to the abbey, which had been splendidly decorated with tapestries, banners and thousands of candles for the occasion. There, Margaret waited in great state, flanked by her entourage, until the Archbishop of Glasgow, who was to perform the ceremony, arrived with an entourage of high ranking Scottish churchmen, followed by King James in his magnificent white and gold wedding clothes, which he wore with a black velvet bonnet decorated with a large, fine ruby rather than his crown. At his side was his brother, the Earl of Ross, while behind the two royal Stewart brothers there processed all of the high nobility of the country, who sat on the right-hand side of the church, leaving the left to Margaret's English entourage. Taking Margaret's hand, James led her into the abbey choir, where they were officially bound together in marriage, after which the Archbishop of York read aloud from the papal bulls that gave permission for the wedding to go ahead, despite the fact that James and Margaret were fourth cousins thanks to James's great-grandmother Joan Beaufort, the wife of James I of Scotland, being the sister of Margaret's great-grandfather John Beaufort, Duke of Somerset. Once these formalities were over, the 'trumpets blew for joy' as James once again took Margaret's hand and led her to the high altar, where they both knelt on plump gold cushions during the orations, litany and Nuptial Mass, after which Margaret was anointed with oil and James solemnly presented her with the royal sceptre of Scotland as a celebratory Te Deum rang out in the lovely old abbey.

Doubtless very relieved that the lengthy wedding ceremony was at an end, Margaret gave her right hand to James and let him lead her from the abbey back to her rooms. They then parted company in order to preside over two separate banquets in their apartments, for which James abandoned his rich wedding outfit and changed into black velvet trimmed with marten fur, while Margaret appears to have continued wearing her wedding clothes. The new queen's banquet took place in her great chamber with the Archbishop of Glasgow, other highly favoured Scottish nobles and her ladies-in-waiting in attendance, while in his own apartments, James hosted a merry company comprising the Earl of Surrey, Bishop of Durham and other gentlemen. Margaret dined from gold plates beneath her cloth-of-gold cloth-of-state at the head of her own separate table, which groaned beneath an enormous amount of food and wine, including a gilded boar's head and a great ham – the first course had twelve dishes, while the second had over forty.

After they had feasted, the couple and their guests met once again in the palace's great hall for the rest of the celebrations. The feasting, music and dancing went on for several hours, and we can well imagine that then as now, the English guests were taken aback by their Scottish neighbours' capacity to have a good time because once they had exhausted themselves dancing, they sat down to yet another elaborate supper. The partying doubtless went on until late in the night, but James and Margaret retired early for their wedding night. Although it was still traditional for newly married royal couples to be accompanied by a noisy entourage of family, courtiers and even high-ranking churchmen, it seems very unlikely that James, hitherto so considerate of his young bride's feelings, would have agreed to such an indignity as a public bedding. Instead, he went off to hear Evensong on his own, while Margaret retired with her ladies in order to prepare for bed and await the arrival of her husband. What happened next is not known, but due to Margaret's youth, it seems likely that James, who had spent so much time kindly reassuring her over the last few days, decided to simply give her a hug and delay the consummation of their marriage until she was older.

Perhaps it was at this moment that James presented his new wife with the exquisitely decorated Book of Hours that now resides in the collection of the Austrian National Library in Vienna. Created in Flanders by some of the most talented miniature painters in Ghent and Bruges, including the master Gerard Horenbout, court painter to Margaret of Austria, who worked on the portrait of James kneeling in prayer before a splendid Gothic altar decorated with his coat of arms, while behind him lurks his patron saint St James the Elder dressed as a pilgrim and holding a staff. Tucked away towards the back of the book there is a companion portrait, possibly also by Horenbout but more likely painted by Clara de Keysere, of Margaret, looking extremely young with red Tudor hair peeping out from beneath her crown, kneeling before a vision of the Virgin Mary with Christ in her arms. The royal arms of the Queen of Scotland decorate Margaret's altar cloth and prayer stool, while a touch of levity is provided by the inclusion of her little white dog, who lies in front of her.

The manuscript remains one of the finest examples of illuminated art and was a precious personal gift for Margaret, not least because it would have been extremely expensive. The Book of Hours was a twelve month calendar of saints days and holy festivals, richly decorated with religious scenes and zodiac symbols while an exquisite profusion of animals, flowers and birds decorates the borders of the pages. Margaret treasured the book for several years before finally parting with it shortly after her husband's death, when she presented it to her younger sister Mary after writing the dedication: 'Madame I pray your grace Remember on me when ye Loke upon thys boke Your lofing syster Margaret' inside. It's not clear why Margaret felt the need to give away her husband's precious gift, but it's possible that it had become a painful reminder of happier times when they were newly married and optimistic about their shared future as King and Queen of Scotland.

Chapter 8

Queen of Scots 1503–1504

The royal wedding was followed by several days of celebrations, including jousting outside the palace, which Margaret and her ladies watched from the windows of her Great Chamber, while James and his gentlemen watched from his apartments next door. Although the English entourage that had accompanied her north of the border were determined not to be impressed by the extravagant wedding festivities, they couldn't help but be swayed by the magnificence of the Scottish court and charisma of its king. Even the conceited Earl of Surrey fell under James's charm and this admiration was clearly reciprocated by the Scottish king   but not by his new wife Margaret, who detested the Earl and his domineering wife. Shortly after her arrival in Scotland she dictated a letter to her father, which was intended to be delivered to him by one of the English ladies returning to London after her wedding, who had, she advised her father, also some verbal messages to be delivered to him, presumably involving matters that she did not dare commit to paper.

After the usual polite greetings, she began by thanking her father for the 'right good attendance' which the household, 'especially to all these ladies and gentlewomen' that he sent with her has given her during her journey north and first few days in Scotland. Clearly her attendants were carefully picked to be both diligent and also comforting at this difficult time and special mention is made of a footman called Thomas, whom she asked her father to reward for his exceptional service:

> Sir, I beseech your Grace to be a good and gracious lord to Thomas, which was footman to the Queen my mother, whose soul God have pardon; for he hath been one of my footmen hither with as great diligence and labour to his great charge of his own good and true mind. I am not able to recompense him, except as a favour of your Grace.

She then moved on to the less pleasant topic of the Earl of Surrey, frostily informing her father that, 'my lord of Surrey is in great favour with the king here and he cannot bear to be without his company at any time of the day'. She then complained that Surrey was interfering in the management of her household and undermining the authority of her Chamberlain, Ralph Verney, who had followed her to Scotland with his wife Eleanor, a half-niece of Lady Margaret Beaufort who had also been one of Elizabeth of York's favourite ladies-in-waiting and was, therefore, a person of some consequence in Margaret's circle. Surrey, she informed her father, 'hath such words unto' Verney whenever he protests against such poor treatment that he 'dare speak no further'. She, however, was determined to speak for him and obviously hoped that her father would intervene and restore harmony to her household.

Although most of the letter has clearly been dictated to a secretary, Margaret decided to take up the pen herself for the last few lines, first apologising for not writing the whole letter herself due to lack of time then adding, rather sadly, that 'I would I were with your Grace now, and many times more'. Clearly the long journey, excitement of meeting her husband for the first time and then the exhausting round of official ceremonies and celebrations for her wedding had taken their toll and left her feeling very far away from home.

The morning after the wedding, James delighted Margaret by presenting her with Kilmarnock in East Ayrshire as the customary 'morrowing gift' that the kings of Scotland gave to their brides on the morning after their wedding. However, welcome though this gift must have been, she was doubtless even more pleased when he announced that the time had come to remove his long auburn beard, which she had made no secret about disliking, and invited Lady Surrey to do the honours and cut it off, assisted by her step daughter Lady Muriel Grey, Viscountess Lisle. Pleased with their efforts, James rewarded the two Howard ladies with a huge pile of expensive fabrics, worth in the region of £500 (roughly £100,000 in modern money) and including all the usual luxuries like silk damask and cloth-of-gold.

The next few weeks would be bittersweet for Margaret as she settled into her new home at the Scottish court and got to know her husband and the people close to him, perhaps even tentatively beginning to forge some friendships of her own with the younger women of the court – although she would never share her mother's happy talent for inspiring enormous loyalty and affection in those close to her. Sadly though, now that the wedding was over, it was time to say goodbye to several familiar faces as most of her

English entourage prepared to return home – a few of Margaret's ladies and household officers would be remaining with her but the majority had no place at the Scottish court and so she was forced to say goodbye as they departed for the border. Among those who remained were Margaret's unnamed lute player, her cornet player and four Italian musicians who had impressed her husband with the fine quality of their playing – the eight minstrels that her father had hired to entertain her during her progress to Scotland were sent home though.

Although Margaret doubtless felt rather sad to be losing most of her English household, including a few people she had known all her life as they had been part of her mother's household, she didn't have much time to mourn their departure before she too was busy preparing to leave Edinburgh. Perhaps thinking that his new wife required distraction, James decided not to delay before taking her on a tour of her chief dower lands, which also happened to comprise some of the most significant royal residences outside Edinburgh. They departed on 18 September, travelling first to the royal pleasure palace of Linlithgow, about fifteen miles west of the capital. There had been a royal residence at Linlithgow since the twelfth century, which had been expanded into a palace by James I after the original manor was destroyed by fire in 1424. Subsequent kings had made minor changes but it was under Margaret's husband James that Linlithgow really flourished. James had always been fond of Linlithgow and was determined to transform it into a modern and sophisticated royal palace, comparable with those in England and on the continent by building opulent new apartments for himself and his consort, adding a beautiful new chapel on the first floor and extending and embellishing the great hall. As with Holyrood, Margaret's imminent arrival inspired James to further embellish Linlithgow, which included adding the entwined initials 'IRM' for James and Margaret to vaulting bosses and floor tiles in the new apartments. There was also a decidedly English style to the new south courtyard front thanks to the arched perpendicular windows, which were very fashionable in England at the time and almost certainly intended as a compliment to the new Queen of Scots. It is no longer known where the queen's apartments were located in Linlithgow, but it seems likely that they were in the now vanished old north range of the palace, adjacent to the king's rooms and following the same sequence of a large hall, presence chamber, bedchamber and oratory for private devotions, along with a wardrobe and closet.

Although the exterior of Linlithgow Palace appears rather austere and even forbidding to modern eyes and, thanks to its current ruined state, it is difficult to imagine how it must have looked in its sixteenth-century heyday, it was considered at the time to be one of the most magnificent royal residences in Scotland and was traditionally regarded as a pleasure palace by the Stewart monarchs – a place where they could retreat to have fun, celebrate, entertain and relax. Always fond of outdoor pursuits, Margaret would have been particularly thrilled by the extensive hunting grounds, well stocked lake and forests that surrounded the palace, while her evenings were filled with music and dancing.

After leaving romantic Linlithgow, the court rode on to Stirling Castle, another one of Margaret's jointure properties and one of particular significance, both historical and political as it commanded one of the most important strategic positions in Scotland from its perch high on a crag of ancient volcanic rock. It was said that to 'hold Stirling, was to hold the country', and Margaret must have felt a thrill of power as she rode through the castle gates, knowing that several of her ancestors had tried and failed to keep Stirling for themselves – most notably Edward II, who lost control of the castle after being defeated by Robert the Bruce at Bannockburn, which was fought within sight of Stirling's ramparts in 1314. It wasn't just a fearsome fortress though and over the past four centuries had been adopted as one of the favourite residences of the Scottish monarchs, who enjoyed not just its almost impenetrable safety but also its many comforts, which included luxurious apartments, lovely gardens, extensive grounds and, slightly further afield but still within close reach, a great hunting park. In short, it had everything that the Scottish kings might feasibly require and in return they lavished it with attention.

James IV was particularly fond of Stirling Castle, not least because he had been born there and spent much of his childhood in the royal nursery which had been established there. It had also been the favourite residence of his beloved mother Margaret of Denmark, and after they became estranged from his father, mother and son lived there together happily, which naturally increased his affection for the castle. He spent a great deal of time there as king and it was the usual location for the court's Easter festivities in the spring. As with the other royal residences, he had spent a great deal of time and money improving Stirling Castle since succeeding to the throne, increasing his efforts when it was confirmed that Margaret would definitely be coming to Scotland in the summer of 1503. James's work at Stirling was significant and radically altered the appearance of the old fortress by adding a splendid new defensive forework and entrance which stood five storeys high and was heavily influenced by the design of French fortresses such as Carcassonne, Bonaguil and Fougères. However, although the massive curtain wall, crenellations and vast, imposing turreted gatehouse all had unquestionable defensive properties and would almost certainly hold their own against any hostile attack, they were also intended to be decorative, to look majestic, even beautiful, and to inspire awe in all who beheld them, whether they be friend or foe – although, sadly, as much of James's forework has now long since vanished it can be difficult to imagine just how magnificent Stirling Castle looked in the early sixteenth century when Margaret Tudor caught her first glimpse of it.

Building work continued at Stirling throughout James's reign and he lavished vast sums on significantly refurbishing the chapel royal and erecting a new residence for himself, which was described in the royal accounts books simply as the 'King's house' and stood on the west side of the castle's inner close. As James was a bachelor when he built his new apartments, he clearly saw no need to commission a matching set of rooms for any future wife and it's still not certain where Margaret would have lodged in Stirling, although it seems likely that she inhabited the old queen's rooms in the original palace, which would later be demolished and entirely replaced by her son James V. It's also highly probable that James invested a great deal of money in remodelling and updating the queen's chambers, adding new modern conveniences and making them even more luxurious. His most important project, just before Margaret's arrival, was the erection of a magnificent new great hall, which was the grandest such structure in Scotland and was inspired by the great hall at Eltham Palace that Margaret had known since childhood.

It was here that the court gathered for banquets, meetings and festivities and in fact the always thoughtful James had provided accommodation in the undercroft for the musicians and theatrical troupes who entertained them. If Margaret had expected the Scottish royal residences to be a bleak and uncomfortable contrast to the luxurious, beautifully decorated Tudor palaces, then she was much surprised and pleased by the sophisticated and modern interiors that James had created in his palaces, as well as the lovely gardens and well-stocked hunting grounds that surrounded them. Unlike her father, who was more concerned with status and display, her husband James took his pleasure very seriously.

However, not everything about Stirling met with Margaret's approval. James had led an eventful life before their marriage (and would discreetly continue to do so afterwards) and it was at Stirling that many of his numerous flirtations had taken place. He had housed Margaret Drummond there before the end of their relationship and his current love, the beguiling Janet Kennedy, had lived there until fairly recently, when he had considered it politic to move her much further away to Darnaway Castle near Forres in Moray – conveniently close to the shrine of Saint Duthac at Tain, which he regularly visited. Although doubtless all evidence of Janet's recent residence had been tactfully removed before Margaret's arrival, no one seems to have considered it necessary to remove the presence of James's numerous illegitimate children, who were housed in the castle's nursery. It's not known how much Margaret was told about her husband's romantic history before she went to Scotland, but it seems probable grandmother Lady Margaret Beaufort would not have allowed her to leave England completely unprepared for what awaited her over the border.

The Tudor court was never as decadent or scandalous as some of its continental contemporaries, most notably the French, and especially so under the aegis of the markedly uxorious Henry VII and his highly moral mother. Obviously though, there would have been talk at the English court about the romantic escapades of the handsome young Scottish king, and this interest in his activities would only have intensified once he became betrothed to the eldest Tudor princess. The question is, how much of this gossip filtered down to his bride to be? What is certain is that Margaret was, understandably, not at all best pleased to find her husband's illegitimate children not only openly residing in Stirling Castle but also doing so in some state. It is to James's credit that he treated his illegitimate offspring with such affection and generosity; an older, more experienced woman might well have thought his behaviour towards them reflected well upon him. Margaret, however, was not quite 14-years-old, spoiled, used to getting her own way, and extremely protective of her own rank and dignity. It is not surprising that she reacted poorly to the presence of her husband's children – the only really surprising thing about the situation is that James had anticipated any other reaction to his great revelation.

Margaret's precise reaction is not known, but she somehow made her husband aware of her displeasure, with the result that the 'royal bairns' were speedily removed from Stirling and packed off to equally splendid establishments elsewhere. The king's 6-year-old daughter, Margaret Stewart, the only child born from his liaison with the doomed Margaret Drummond, was set up with her own household in Edinburgh Castle, where she was treated like a princess. This can't have pleased her father's new wife all that much either, but even Margaret seems to have known where to draw the line; the girl's new household was left undisturbed until she left seven years later to marry John Gordon, second son of the Earl of Huntly. Meanwhile, James's sons were also being raised in a most princely manner with every trapping that cherished Renaissance princes could require. The eldest boy, Alexander Stewart, the son of James's first significant mistress Marion Boyd, was particularly loved by his father, who intended him for a career in the church and would, a year later, have him made Archbishop of Saint Andrews at the tender age of just 11-years-old.

Keen to ensure that his son would have the best education, and perhaps feeling wistful that he himself had rarely managed to leave Scotland, James would later send Alexander abroad on a lengthy European trip which anticipated the Grand Tours taken by young aristocrats in the eighteenth century. The high point of this odyssey through the European centres of culture and learning was being tutored in ancient Greek and rhetoric by the great Erasmus himself in Padua. Erasmus was taken with the young Scottish princeling, who had inherited all of his father's charm as well as his intellectual curiosity and talent for languages and music, and would later fondly recall their time together in the eulogy that he wrote for Alexander after Flodden, making it clear that he had been as impressed by the son of James IV as he had been by the young Henry VIII.

Perhaps Margaret was better pleased by another resident of Stirling Castle – the Italian born alchemist John Damian, who had been installed in the castle and provided with a fully equipped laboratory by the king. James was fascinated by science and medicine and tasked Damian with the job of discovering the celebrated Philosopher's Stone, which was believed to become transformed into the miraculous Elixir of Life and have the ability to cure all ills when mixed with wine. James squandered a great deal of money both on Damian's experiments and also his apparently endless appetite for whisky. A few years later, in 1507, Damian entertained the court by conducting an ill-fated experiment with flight, which involved jumping from the top of Stirling Castle equipped only with feathered wings. Sadly, and rather predictably, it ended in disaster but fortunately for Damian he got off relatively lightly with a broken thigh bone and lived to see another day. As James was inordinately proud of his alchemist, there can be no doubt that he introduced him to Margaret and perhaps she was even favoured with a tour of Master Damian's mysterious laboratory.

After leaving Stirling, the royal cavalcade continued on to the modest but lovely palace of Falkland in Fife, which had been a pretty domestic castle until James began to transform it into a small but perfectly formed royal residence with a distinctly French ambience. Built on a much smaller scale than any of the other Scottish palaces that Margaret had hitherto visited, staying there was a much more intimate event, with the royal couple and their entourage inhabiting relatively small apartments. However, this state of affairs was more than compensated for by the palace's enviable location, surrounded by magnificent countryside and, more importantly as far as the hunting-mad Stewarts were concerned, miles of dense forests filled with game. After leaving Falkland Palace, the royal party continued north to Scone Abbey in Perthshire, a place with important royal associations, where they lodged in the abbot's palace. Like all Kings of Scotland, James had been crowned at Scone on 24 June 1488, less than a fortnight after his father's death after the Battle of Sauchieburn, and the site would always hold a deep significance for him. Unfortunately, the famous Stone of Destiny, which had formerly been used as a throne at the coronation of Scottish kings had been stolen from Scone by Edward I of England in 1296 and would not be returned to Scotland until 1996. It was clearly very important to James that Margaret should visit Scone as soon as possible after their marriage and it is likely that they both found the experience very moving – although Margaret may well have felt some awkwardness about the fact that her father retained possession of the Stone of Destiny.

By the end of October, the royal couple were back at Linlithgow Palace, where they were to spend three weeks enjoying the hunting and last warm days of autumn before returning to Edinburgh, where they were to celebrate Margaret's fourteenth birthday at the end of November and then Christmas. Both events were marked by all the usual festivities, which gave Margaret more opportunities to compare her husband's young and fun-loving court with that of her rather more staid and status-obsessed father. The Tudor court was one of the most magnificent in Europe, especially now that Henry VII's great palace at Richmond was completed and in use, but Margaret's father was hampered by a vague feeling of insecurity rooted in his tenuous claim to the throne; this manifested itself in a need to exert his authority at all times and to never allow the mask of kingship to slip as he boosted his family's prestige with displays of royal magnificence designed to forcefully underline his right to the throne.

On the other hand, his son-in-law, James of Scotland, was the latest in a long line of Stewart kings and the undisputed legitimate heir to a crown that had been worn by his father and grandfather before him. He had absolutely nothing to prove and his fun-loving, laid-back court was a reflection of this. Although there can be no doubt that Margaret missed

England and her family, she was quickly learning to appreciate the youthful, carefree atmosphere at the Scottish court. Certainly she could have had no complaints about her extravagant birthday celebrations, which involved all the usual feasting, dancing, music and jousting outside Holyrood Palace. Her first Christmas in Scotland was even more lavish, and no doubt a lot of fun as well, as the Scots threw themselves into the annual revelries which marked the end of one year and beginning of the next. The entertainments were organised by James's alchemist John Damian, who was appointed Master of the Revels for the occasion and wholeheartedly devoted himself into his task, making that year's Christmas one of the most memorable ever held at the Scottish court. Perhaps the doctor's knowledge of science came in handy when planning the mummeries that were an integral part of a sixteenth-century royal Yuletide as he would have been able to provide some rudimentary pyrotechnics and other special effects.

For Margaret, 1503 had been the momentous year of her life as it had seen her marry, become a queen, lose her beloved mother and then leave behind everything and everyone she knew in order to travel hundreds of miles to begin a new life in a different country. We don't know how Margaret felt as she sat in state in the new great hall at Holyrood Palace with her husband at her side and surveyed their courtiers enjoying the Christmas festivities, which included plays, 'moorish' dancing, plenty of silly pranks and dressing up, but we can hope that she felt reasonably contented with the cards that had been dealt to her. At least she had no reason to complain about the gifts that her husband presented to her on New Year's Day, which was the traditional day to exchange presents in the beginning of the sixteenth century. The presentation of these presents was a serious business at this time and was an opportunity for courtiers to make a good impression, and for members of the royal family to show favour to those fortunate enough to have pleased them during the last twelve months. James was obviously feeling extremely pleased with how his year had gone for he was remarkably generous with his presents that year, giving Margaret a 'heavy ducat' of gold which weighed a whole ounce and then the next day adding two gold rings set with sapphires and two crosses studded with pearls to her jewellery collection.

Perhaps of more value to Margaret was the great attention that her husband showed towards her during the Christmas celebrations – he was always very kind but he was especially attentive that winter, making a point of partnering her whenever she wished to dance and sitting at her table when they played cards. Always naturally ebullient, James was on top form that December – but his good mood came to an abrupt end when his only surviving brother James, Duke of Ross, died suddenly in early 1504. Although their difficult father James III had done his best to separate the brothers, and even pit them against each other, they had nonetheless remained close and James was genuinely distressed by this unexpected loss. The blow of Ross's death was compounded by the fact that he had been heir presumptive to the throne, which made it important that James and Margaret produce a legitimate heir as soon as possible to prevent the throne passing out of the hands of the direct Stewart line to the new heir presumptive, James's first cousin, John Stewart, Duke of Albany.

Whether by accident or design, over two years would pass before Margaret fulfilled her duty by conceiving a child and securing the succession. In the meantime, James continued to cherish his illegitimate children, even raising a few eyebrows by bestowing his dead brother's Archbishopric of Saint Andrews, one of the richest and most important church positions in Scotland, on his eldest son, Alexander Stewart (which had the additional benefit of meaning that the rich revenues of the demesne of Saint Andrews would end up in the crown's coffers until Alexander was old enough to be properly consecrated). Margaret can hardly have been pleased about the boy being shown such a signal honour, but there was very little she could do until she had strengthened her position by bearing a child of her own.

Chapter 9

The Little Queen 1504–1509

On the 13 March 1504, seven months after his wedding, James IV took the seat of honour beneath his cloth of state in the Parliament Hall of Edinburgh's old Tolbooth building, where the Scottish Parliament met during the sixteenth century. The official record of John Murray, the notary who recorded the occasion for posterity states that 'our most dread lord', King James, was 'royally robed and clothed, the crown on his head, bearing the royal sceptre in his hand' as he sat in judgement, surrounded by 'the prelates, barons, freeholders and commissioners of the burghs, representing the three estates of his realm, universally summoned from each province [and] part and assembled at that place', which included the highest churchmen and noblemen of Scotland. Margaret was apparently absent from this gathering of the most important men of Scotland, even though some of that day's Parliamentary business chiefly concerned her.

Although the spiritual nature of her queenship had been underlined by her anointing during the wedding ceremony at Holyrood Abbey the previous August, it was now time for her husband's Parliament to acknowledge the more temporal and official nature of her role by ratifying and confirming the many valuable gifts and grants of crown land that had been given to her as part of the marriage treaty he had signed on 24 May 1503 before her arrival in Scotland. There was also a special mention for the lordship and castle of Kilmarnock, which James had presented to Margaret the morning after her wedding and which was now confirmed to belong to her for the rest of her life.

By the time the first anniversary of her marriage came around, Margaret must have felt like she was at last beginning to understand the complicated, fascinating, erudite man she had married. They divided most of the first half of the year between Holyrood Palace, where they spent a riotous Easter, Linlithgow and Stirling, in a pattern that would be repeated throughout the rest of their marriage – their visits dictated as much by James's restless nature as by the need to keep moving between residences so that they could be thoroughly cleaned between visits. Although the royal apartments were luxuriously decorated and well furnished, the couple still travelled with an enormous baggage train of goods, which included more personal items like books, musical instruments, James's collection of tools and medical equipment (his accounts refer to the purchase of dentistry tools, which he occasionally used on hapless courtiers – to be fair to James though, the accounts also make it plain that he paid his patients rather than vice versa) and clothes, as well as cartloads of furniture and the all-important precious tapestries that accompanied them between residences and were ceremoniously hammered into place the moment the king arrived.

It was an enormous and exhausting enterprise to keep the royal court moving between the various palaces and a great deal of energy was expended in ensuring that the operation was as seamless and incident free as possible – not that Margaret would have noticed this as she played no part in the preparations, packing and unpacking, other than to perhaps stipulate that a favoured item of clothing should be brought along for the trip. However, while Margaret was apparently content to remain within a short distance of Edinburgh, her husband was far more intrepid and continued his practice of travelling to every corner of his country, often covering vast distances in one day depending on the weather and riding conditions.

In the spring of 1504, James rode to the Highlands, a journey of over 160 miles, in order to visit his mistress Janet Kennedy, who had fallen seriously ill and wasn't responding to the treatment ministered by the royal doctor he had sent to her. Tactfully, the king informed his wife that he was going north to visit the shrine of his beloved St Duthac in Tain, but everyone knew that his trip had an ulterior purpose. James's interest in St Duthac was nonetheless genuine though, and Margaret would definitely have realised by now that her husband was extremely devout – as evidenced by his punctilious attendance at Mass and the close attention that he paid to the refurbishment of the chapels in his various residences. Perhaps by now she had even caught a glimpse of James's famous cilice, the heavy linked chain that he wore around his waist in penance for his involvement in the overthrow and violent death of his father James III after the battle of Sauchieburn in June 1488. James, just 15-years-old at the time, had been alienated from his father by his clear preference for his younger brother and was manipulated by a cohort of nobles keen to use him as a figurehead while they wrought his father's downfall. In reality, due to his youth, James had very little to reproach himself for but even so, he continued to deeply regret his involvement for the rest of his life.

After spending June at Linlithgow Palace, where they enjoyed hunting and boating on the loch, the couple moved on to Stirling for the rest of the summer. The restless James was soon off again though, this time to the borders region where he teamed up with Lord Dacre to deal with a disruptive flurry of thieving. Although his marriage to Margaret had done much to calm the centuries-long rivalry that had made the borders area such a hotbed of violence and crime, there was still plenty of work to be done. Unlike many of his regal peers who preferred to maintain a distance between themselves and their subjects, James enjoyed spending as much time as possible with his people and had the same highly involved, hands-on approach to kingship that his ancestors had employed. Whereas King Henry rarely left the vicinity of London and was not personally involved in the dispensing of justice (although it was under his aegis that the Star Chamber court was instituted at the Palace of Westminster), James thought nothing of travelling all over his country in order to preside over trials in the local courts, known as ayres, and make judgements.

His journey south in the summer of 1504 was particularly successful, although perhaps rather less so for the captured wrongdoers, many of whom were hanged. Pleased with the outcome, James rewarded himself with three weeks of hawking before making his way to Dunfermline, where he was due to meet up with his wife. Dunfermline was one of the oldest royal residences in Scotland and there had been a palace there since the eleventh century when Malcolm III made the town his capital, while the neighbouring abbey was founded a generation later and was by now one of the most significant religious sites in the country. James had turned his attention to the royal apartments at the start of the sixteenth century and they were particularly magnificent, although perhaps still a little old fashioned. However, if Margaret expected her husband to remain with her for any length of time then she was doomed to disappointment, for within less than a week he had gone again, this time to the very north of the country.

That year's Christmas court was once again held at Holyrood Palace, with Margaret and James presiding over all of the usual revelries. Perhaps it was during this court celebration that James embarked on his latest affair with a young woman mysteriously referred to as 'L of A' in his accounts. James may have been lavishing gifts on his new mistress, but he was still as generous as ever towards his wife. Margaret clearly felt the cold, and the royal household accounts have several references to new gowns, jewels and costly furs, which were used to trim her dresses during the frosty winter months. Although James paid Margaret's expenses, he had doubtless been relieved when her father sent the second instalment of her dowry in the summer of 1505, along with an extra 5,000 gold marks to cover his daughter's expenses. Perhaps word had reached him in London of Margaret's extravagance as she battled boredom and homesickness and established herself in her new position.

Nonetheless, however much Margaret spent on dresses and trinkets was a drop in the ocean compared with the vast sums, mostly drawn from her dowry, that her husband was spending on the establishment of a new Scottish navy, which was to be his primary obsession for the rest of his life and would ultimately become one of the greatest achievements of his reign. During 1505, he was preoccupied with the new ships he had ordered, which included two huge warships: the *Margaret*, which was obviously named for his wife; and a 1,000-ton flagship, the *Great Michael*, which was not just the largest ship in his new navy, but also one of the biggest in Europe. Like the previous year, while her husband travelled extensively around his country, Margaret remained close to Edinburgh, spending much of her time at her favourite residence, Linlithgow Palace.

The couple were together for all of the main religious festivals, which were spent at Holyrood Palace that year. On Shrove Tuesday, the day before the annual Easter fast began, there was a day of revels and feasting at the Scottish court during which James paid several African musicians to play for the court, including a drummer who pleased him so much that he retained him and bought him a horse so that he could accompany him on his travels around the country. Also performing that day was an energetic troupe of twelve dancers who were dressed in black and white costumes; they delighted Margaret so much that she joined in and ended up having a nosebleed thanks to her exertions.

Margaret's health had never been very robust, and the nosebleed caused enough concern for a court physician to be consulted and a 'blood stone', another name for jasper, which was believed to have the ability to staunch bleeding, to be purchased for the young queen. Overall though her health remained good until the summer of 1506, when her first pregnancy was announced, to the delight and joy of everyone – except perhaps the Duke of Albany who now stood in danger of losing the position of heir presumptive to the Scottish throne. It is not known when Margaret and her husband consummated their marriage but it seems likely that James, always gentlemanly when it came to matters of the heart, had taken on board the understandable concerns of her grandmother Lady Margaret Beaufort, who believed herself to have been permanently damaged by the physical trauma of bearing a child when she was still only in her early teens, and had therefore waited until his bride turned 16 in November 1505 before doing the deed. The fact that after this first successful conception, Margaret would go on to get pregnant almost every year, would also support this theory as it makes it clear that the couple had no fertility issues once they got started.

James was naturally delighted to finally have a legitimate heir on the way, while Margaret was pleased and relieved to have done her duty and strengthened the bond between England and Scotland. The couple were closer than ever that summer as they looked forward to the birth of their child and in June, Margaret accompanied James on a trip aboard his newly finished warship the *Margaret* from Leith to the Isle of May in the Firth of Forth. The Isle was the site of one of the earliest Christian churches in Scotland and therefore a place of special veneration to the devout king, who spent their visit deep in conversation with an acetic hermit who lived there, while Margaret prayed at a chapel devoted to Saint Adrian of May, a priest who was murdered by Viking raiders along with all the other inhabitants of the monastery there. The peaceful, isolated island was popular with pilgrims and it had become the custom for visitors to place a stone from the beach on a cairn there. It's likely that James and Margaret did so too before taking their leave from the island and returning to the mainland.

They spent much of the summer of 1506 at the Palace of Linlithgow as usual. It was perhaps the happiest time they had spent together since their marriage – and was no doubt made all the sweeter by the arrival in August of the third and final instalment of Margaret's dowry, much of which would go towards James's great warship the *Great Michael*, which was currently under construction at the new dock in Newhaven. For James, who was so ambitious for his country, this great ship was symbolic of Scotland's independence, strength and ability to defend itself against its enemies. However, more than that, it was also intended as a means for him to prove himself, for by 1506, doubtless spurred on by his wife's pregnancy and the fact that he might at last gain a legitimate heir, James had already decided that he wanted to lead a new crusade to Jerusalem and he would do so in the *Great Michael*. Although this desire to become a Crusader King was definitely primarily inspired by his guilt over his father's death and constant desire to expiate himself, it was also a natural result of James's longing to really place himself and his country on the map, to make Scotland relevant in Europe and enhance his own prestige and importance as the perfect chivalric prince, who was both a man of God as well as a skilled military tactician. To this end, he despatched an envoy to Venice at the end of 1506 to request the help of the Doge, which was duly given. What Margaret thought of all this is not known – James's departure to the Holy Land would potentially leave her alone for several years and if her husband failed to return, like so many men who went on a crusade to the Holy Land, then she might well find herself either running the country as regent for their child or, even worse, packed off back to England.

Excited by the prospect of imminent fatherhood and hoping to cheer up Margaret who, like a lot of women, found the third trimester of pregnancy exhausting, boring and extremely uncomfortable, James paid for sixty-nine musicians to play for his court during that year's Christmas festivities at Holyrood Palace. Margaret may not have been able to dance, but she could never resist good music and this thoughtful gesture on the part of her husband would no doubt have done much to improve her spirits as her pregnancy dragged on. She was still at Holyrood when she went into labour and gave birth to her first child on 21 February 1507. To the delight of everyone, the baby was a boy, the longed for male heir, who was named James and given the title Duke of Rothesay as was traditional for the eldest son of the king. As was customary, James was not present at the birth, but he rewarded the female servant who gave him the news of the new arrival with a silver goblet filled to the rim with gold coins.

The baby prince was christened two days later in Holyrood Abbey, borne to the font on an ermine-trimmed cloth-of-gold cushion and dressed in white silk. However, while the court celebrated the arrival of an heir to the throne, his mother lay dangerously ill in her bedchamber upstairs. It had not been an easy labour and Margaret, who was just 17 and had lost her mother to the horrors of childbirth only a few years earlier, suffered a great deal and fell into a fever immediately afterwards – a very worrying symptom at a time when women regularly succumbed to childbed fevers and died. Although he was not passionately in love with his wife, James cared enough about her to make a pilgrimage on foot to the shrine devoted to Saint Ninian 120 miles away in Whithorn Priory, Dumfries and Galloway. The arduous journey took seven days to complete with the desperately worried king walking every step of the way without complaint – the band of four Italian musicians he had taken with him were less stoical about their sore feet though and eventually had to be sent back on hastily hired horses, while their royal master pressed on to the shrine.

It would later be claimed that Margaret began to recover the instant her husband fell to his knees before the shrine of Saint Ninian but although it makes for a lovely story, and one that would have been particularly pleasing to the devout King James, it is unlikely to be true. However, whatever the reason – whether divine, medical or simply luck – Margaret did indeed begin to recover a few weeks after her son's birth and by the end of spring was appearing in public once again. During her convalescence, on Easter Sunday, 4 April, Antonio Inviziati, a Vatican emissary sent by Pope Julius II appeared at court and presented the delighted James with a bejewelled sword of state and a purple velvet cap embellished with gold leaves as a token of the Pope's approval of the Scottish king's plan to lead a new crusade into the Holy Land. Margaret would have looked on in pride as later that same day, James Beaton, Abbot of Dunfermline placed the cap on James's head and the sword in his hand as he knelt before the great altar of Holyrood Abbey.

For James, this tangible signal of Papal approval would have been deeply moving and would, in part at least, have gone some way to absolve him of the guilt he felt about his part in his father's overthrow and death. It also made him more determined to complete the *Great Michael*, which was by now the envy of all Europe, with even Louis XII of France expressing his jealousy, no doubt much to James's pleasure. It was an expensive enterprise though and now that he had no more instalments of Margaret's dowry to look forward to, James was forced to look about for more sources of income to fund his passion for ship-building. There were other costs too, for the great enterprise was denuding his kingdom's forests at an alarming rate as foresters struggled to keep up with the demand for timber.

Meanwhile, the baby Duke of Rothesay continued to thrive and in June, after several months of preparation, James mounted an ambitious and extravagant tournament to celebrate not just the arrival of his much longed for son and heir, but also the recovery of his wife from the ordeals of childbirth. The pageant was entitled 'The Jousting of the Wild Knight and the Black Lady', and revolved around the person of a young Moorish woman known at court as Black Ellen, who had been brought to Scotland with another girl at the end of 1504 by one of James's sea captains Robert Barton, who presented them to Margaret as gifts.

By all accounts, both Margaret and James were very fond of Black Ellen and Black Margaret and the former's beauty in particular seems to have caused quite a stir at their court, which makes it unsurprising that she was chosen to act as the heroine of the royal pageant. James was passionately fond of tournaments but this one had an additional twist of involving a delightful romantic narrative according to which the Wild Knight, naturally played by James himself and accompanied by an entourage of 'wild men' dressed in goat skins with antlers attached to their helmets, took on all challengers for the hand of the Black Lady on jousting lists that had been specially erected at the foot of Edinburgh Castle. We have the often irreverent court poet William Dunbar to thank for a detailed description of the event as he recorded it all for posterity in his poem 'Ane Blak More', assigning the starring role to his patron King James, while describing the Black Lady herself in rather less flattering terms as 'My Lady with the muckle lips' – a reference to her full lips, which winners would be entitled to kiss. The tournament lasted for five weeks and was by all accounts a most glorious affair, with no expense spared to create a wonderful and colourful spectacle.

The tournament was heavily inspired by old tales of the exploits of King Arthur and his knights, which were considered the pinnacle of chivalric perfection at the beginning of the sixteenth century. Alongside the jousting lists there was a huge, brightly coloured silk pavilion, where the ladies of the court could shield themselves from the sun, and several smaller ones where the knights could prepare for their sport and engage in some of the usual male swaggering with their squires and friends. There was also a rather fancifully named Garden of Patience, home to the Tree of Hope, from which sprouted the Fruits of Honour, Leaves of Pleasure and Flowers of Nobility, and upon whose branches a shield bearing the arms of that week's challenger was hung for all to see.

The participants were lavishly dressed for the occasion, with James sporting a fearsome-looking horned black helmet and costume that had been procured for him in London, while the Black Lady wore a beautiful gold, patterned, damask gown trimmed with yellow and green taffeta and made her grand entrance sitting in a gold litter, draped with an extravagant 160 metres of fine Flemish taffeta. On the last night of the pageant, the night sky over Edinburgh Castle rippled with fireworks in what was the first instance of pyrotechnics ever staged in Scotland. It's easy to imagine James and his alchemist John Damian taking a personal interest in the creation of these fireworks, which were chiefly made from fireballs and quicksilver. The tournament was so well received by the court and people that James repeated it the following year when he was visited by two high-ranking French envoys sent by Louis XII in order to court James's support for the League of Cambrai, which had been set up to curb the influence of Venice in northern Italy.

As a contrast to all the noisy excitement and bombast of her husband's grand pageant, Margaret gave her own, much quieter, thanks for the birth of her child and followed in her husband's footsteps to the shrine of St Ninian at Whithorn as soon as she felt strong enough to leave Edinburgh. However, unlike James, she did not travel by foot but was instead conveyed by litter, accompanied by seventeen pack horses laden with all the luggage that such an enterprise required. Due to the rest stops considered necessary along the way it took her a month to reach Whithorn and then another month to return home. Although Margaret would never be as devout as her husband, and could even be relatively dilatory when it came to her religious observances, she still had a simple faith in the potency of holy relics and believed that directly communing with the saints, either in their shrines or by handling objects that were allegedly connected to them, was perhaps more effective than simple prayer alone. Sadly though, even the mystical powers of Saint Ninian were not enough to save Prince James when he fell seriously ill at Stirling Castle in February 1508 and then died just six days after his first birthday.

Margaret and James were naturally distraught to have lost their son, but no doubt consoled themselves with the fact that she was already five months pregnant with a baby that had been conceived in early October 1507. They were still grieving the loss of their son when they were informed that James's cousins, the Earl of Arran and his brother Patrick Hamilton, had been arrested while travelling through England without a letter of safe conduct on their way back from escorting James's eldest son to France to continue his education there. Relations between James and his father-in-law had been somewhat strained for some time, primarily because Henry suspected James of retaining some loyalty to the 'Auld Alliance' that had existed for generations between Scotland and England's old enemy France, and was concerned that he might eventually throw his lot in with the French. Thanks to his network of informants, he knew for a fact that the Earl of Arran had been negotiating with King Louis and so decided to strike back by detaining the Earl and preventing him from returning to Scotland, claiming that his activities in France were in violation of the Treaty of Perpetual Peace that had been signed at the time of James's marriage to Henry's daughter Margaret. If Henry had intended to provoke James then he definitely succeeded, for his normally calm and even-tempered son-in-law was absolutely furious about what he saw as an inexcusable affront both to him and his family.

Perhaps realising that he had gone too far, Henry responded by despatching one of his new chaplains, a rising star and formidable politician called Thomas Wolsey, to Scotland to talk sense into James and try to sniff out what was actually going on. If Wolsey was expecting a warm welcome from the famously charming King of Scotland, he was seriously disappointed by what awaited him in Edinburgh once he had belatedly received permission from James to cross the border at Berwick. He arrived on 28 March, somewhat bemused to realise that everyone seemed to know why he was there thanks to the speed with which gossip travelled in court circles and beyond, and was immediately granted an audience with Margaret, who did her best to defuse the tense situation that was brewing but was too inexperienced to be effective. The best she could do was promise to arrange a meeting between Wolsey and her husband, but even there she proved ineffectual because another five days passed before James, who had claimed to be too 'busy shooting guns and making gunpowder' to see him, agreed to an audience. The two men continued to meet every day for over a week, during which time James veered between ranting about the perfidy of the English, complaining about the pressure that many of his nobles were putting on him to renew the Auld Alliance with the French and also, more gratifyingly as far as King Henry was concerned, expressing his gratitude for the diplomatic opportunities that his marriage to Margaret had given him.

Wolsey sent a lengthy despatch back to London, detailing their meetings and giving a full account of his conversations with James, whom he clearly found both intellectually fascinating and also deeply confusing due to James's wily tongue and 'inconstancy'. Of Margaret, King Henry's daughter, he had very little to say other than to note that she did her best to defend her father against accusations that he had maltreated Arran and his brother – which caused some awkwardness as everyone knew that it was Patrick Hamilton himself who had told James about their poor treatment in England.

Meanwhile, the unfortunate Wolsey wryly informed his master that the Scottish court was rife with antipathy towards the English and mostly in favour of an alliance with the French. He had even, he reported, been told to his face that 'no one was ever less welcome in Scotland' than he, thanks to his clear determination to dissuade James from this apparently much-longed-for alliance with France. In the end though, thanks in part to Wolsey's diplomatic skills, the crisis was averted, Arran was returned to Scotland, the Auld Alliance was left to gather dust and some level of cordiality was restored to relations between James and his father-in-law, who sent him a present of some horses and in return received hunting hawks and some Galloway ponies – a now extinct but at the time much prized breed known for its strength and hardiness.

Margaret Tudor, Daniel Mytens, c. 1620–38, Royal Collection Trust / © Her
Majesty Queen Elizabeth II 2018

The Family of Henry
VII with St George and
the Dragon, unknown
artist, c. 1503–9, Royal
Collection Trust /
© Her Majesty Queen
Elizabeth II 2018

Henry VII, unknown
artist, c. 1550–1699,
Royal Collection Trust /
© Her Majesty Queen
Elizabeth II 2018

Elizabeth of York, unknown artist,
c. 1470–98, Royal Collection Trust /
© Her Majesty Queen Elizabeth II
2018

Margaret Beaufort, unknown
artist, c. 1550–1650,
Royal Collection Trust /
© Her Majesty Queen
Elizabeth II 2018

Arthur Tudor, unknown artist, c. 1520, Royal Collection Trust / © Her Majesty
Queen Elizabeth II 2018

Mary Tudor, Queen of France, after Jean Perréal, Royal Collection Trust / © Her Majesty Queen Elizabeth II 2018

Henry VIII as a young boy, Guido Mazzoni, c. 1498, Royal Collection Trust / © Her Majesty Queen Elizabeth II 2018

Henry VIII, Lucas
Horenbout, c. 1526,
Royal Collection Trust /
© Her Majesty Queen
Elizabeth II 2018

Catherine of Aragon,
Wenceslas Hollar, 1652,
Royal Collection Trust /
© Her Majesty Queen
Elizabeth II 2018

Westminster Hall, after George Hawkins, 1801, Royal Collection Trust /
© Her Majesty Queen Elizabeth II 2018

Lambeth Palace, after Leonard Knyff, Royal Collection Trust / © Her Majesty Queen Elizabeth II 2018

Richmond Palace, James Basire, Royal Collection Trust / © Her Majesty Queen Elizabeth II 2018

James IV, miniature by Gugliemo Faija, 1848, Royal Collection Trust / © Her Majesty Queen Elizabeth II 2018

James IV, engraving by unknown artist, 1796, Royal Collection Trust / © Her Majesty Queen Elizabeth II 2018

Holyrood Palace, John Gellatly, Royal Collection Trust / © Her Majesty Queen Elizabeth II 2018

Holyrood Abbey, David Roberts, 1823, Royal Collection Trust / © Her Majesty
Queen Elizabeth II 2018

Above: Stirling Castle,
William Leighton Leitch,
Royal Collection Trust /
© Her Majesty Queen
Elizabeth II 2018

Right: Archibald Douglas,
6th Earl of Angus,
unknown artist, c. 1500–99,
Royal Collection Trust /
© Her Majesty Queen
Elizabeth II 2018

JOHN DUKE OF ALBANY

QUEEN MARGARET

From a Picture in the Possession of the Marquis of Bute to whom this plate is respectfully inscribed by his most Obed.t serv.t

Above: Engraving of Margaret Tudor and John Stewart, Duke of Albany, unknown artist, 1798, Royal Collection Trust / © Her Majesty Queen Elizabeth II 2018

Left: Cardinal Wolsey, after Hans Holbein the Younger, Royal Collection Trust / © Her Majesty Queen Elizabeth II 2018

Marie de Guise, unknown artist c. 1600, Royal Collection Trust / © Her Majesty
Queen Elizabeth II 2018

Lady Margaret Douglas, Countess of Lennox, unknown artist, c. 1572, Royal Collection Trust / © Her Majesty Queen Elizabeth II 2018

Naturally the couple hoped that Margaret's second pregnancy would result in another boy to replace the one that had died, but once again they were doomed to disappointment for at Holyrood Palace on 15 July, Margaret gave birth to a stillborn daughter, whose name was not recorded for posterity. Once again the young queen, who was still just 18-years-old, suffered terribly during her labour and became extremely ill afterwards. Even when she had physically recovered from her ordeal, her fragile and depressed emotional state gave rise to so much concern that James felt he had no option but to remove her from the noise and bustle of court life and instal her at the small, but nonetheless stately, Falkland Palace in Fife, where she could recuperate at her leisure.

The royal couple remained at Falkland for six months before returning to Holyrood Palace in January 1509, where they would have been informed that Margaret's father was grievously ill. This may not have been cause for any great concern though – King Henry had been ailing for a number of years and was especially prone to falling ill over the winter, when the cold and damp weather aggravated his asthma and weak chest, bringing on attacks of pleurisy. He had been thought close to death's door a couple of years earlier but had recovered so it was no doubt hoped, by the few who loved him at least, that he would once again pull through. Sadly though, despite the prayers of his family, Henry VII passed away at his beloved Richmond Palace on 21 April 1509. He was 52-years-old and had reigned for almost twenty-four years. Although he had become increasingly unpopular in his later years, thanks to the crippling new taxes he introduced, there was still no doubt in anyone's minds that he had brought peace and prosperity to a country that had been brought to its knees by decades of civil war and instability. The new King of England was Margaret's 17-year-old younger brother, who would take the throne as Henry VIII. Untried, untested, and barely known outside court circles, everyone waited with bated breath to find out just what sort of king Henry would prove to be.

Chapter 10

The Auld Alliance 1509–1513

While Margaret had been adjusting to her new life in Scotland, life had gone on without her back in England and although she was kept appraised of the latest family news thanks to the letters of her father and grandmother, she still must have felt cut off and, occasionally, even abandoned by her family. In many respects she was far more fortunate than many princesses of her time, who found themselves being sent thousands of miles away from home in order to marry much older, uncongenial men who spoke a different language and were possibly also as unhappy about the match as they were. Margaret, in contrast, had been lucky enough to be sent just 400 miles to marry a handsome, intelligent, charming man who shared the same language (more or less – allowing for Scottish dialect) and clearly cared a great deal about her wellbeing. She was still desperately homesick for some time after her first arrival in Scotland and although it would have been an easy enough matter to cross the border that divided them, there doesn't seem to have been talk of anyone from her family visiting her in Edinburgh, or of her returning home to see them – not even for special occasions like the betrothal of her sister, funeral of her father or coronation of her brother Henry VIII. Instead, she was forced to experience her family's activities vicariously through their letters and there can be no doubt, based on what we know of Margaret's character, that this would often have rankled.

Through these family letters and official despatches sent from London to Scotland, she would have learned of her father's increasingly poor health and his attempts to ally himself in marriage either with Archduchess Margaret, the daughter of Emperor Maximilian I, or her widowed sister-in-law, Juana of Castile, who was also the elder sister of Catherine of Aragon. Reading between the lines, she would have gleaned that her father was not entirely confident about what sort of king her brother Henry would be, and that as a result he kept the boy as close as possible, obviously afraid to let him get close to any of the court factions. Her sister Mary, who was the uncontested star of the court in Margaret's absence, might have written excited letters to tell her about the arrangements for her magnificent betrothal to the Archduke Charles, son of Juana of Castile and heir to his grandfather Maximilian I's vast empire and fortune, and maybe she joined in the general disappointment when the marriage, which would have been a brilliant coup for the whole Tudor family, eventually failed to materialise. Perhaps she even received letters from her former sister-in-law, Catherine of Aragon, who had remained in England since Prince Arthur's untimely death in 1502, expecting to be betrothed to his younger brother Henry, but instead becoming an unwilling pawn in an extended stand off between her father and King Henry, which had resulted in her becoming increasingly estranged from court, abandoned by former friends and living in a state of genteel poverty because she had been left to shoulder her household expenses all by herself while her future fate hung in the balance. Letters are no real substitute for actually spending time with people though and as the years went by, Margaret must have felt increasingly left out.

On 11 June 1509, King Henry married his brother's widow, Catherine of Aragon, claiming that it had been his father's final wish that he do so and less than a fortnight later, on the 24 June, the couple were crowned King and Queen of England in a magnificent ceremony in Westminster Abbey. Margaret was absent from the celebrations but her younger sister Mary, who was now officially referred to as the Princess of Castile since her betrothal to the Archduke Charles, took a prominent part in the coronation festivities at the side of her grandmother, Lady Margaret Beaufort, who openly wept for joy to see a second Tudor king on the throne of England.

Although Margaret and James were absent from the celebrations, they still cast a long shadow over the event because everyone present was well aware that until Henry and Catherine produced a child of their own, Margaret was now first in line to the throne behind her brother and there was every possibility that a Stuart might one day inherit the crown that the Tudors had schemed so hard to get their hands on. As Catherine was still just 24-years-old and came from famously fecund stock, there was no real need to panic; even so, the newlyweds must have felt some pressure to start filling the royal nursery as quickly as possible. In the meantime, relations between the English and Scottish royal houses remained cordial with Henry writing to James shortly after his succession and James replying with a letter of congratulation on 11 June, in which he professes himself 'glad to understand the good will which the king bears him', and promises to 'bear the same towards him', which kickstarted an exchange of friendly missives between the two brothers-in-law. In many ways, Henry and James had a lot in common – they were both intelligent, energetic, restless, charismatic and cultured, but unlike his even-tempered Scottish counterpart, Henry was quick to anger, prone to paranoia, selfish and capable of almost unbelievable ruthlessness. Although things seemed to be going well now, it was only a matter of time before it ended in disaster.

There was more tragedy for the Tudor family when the matriarch, Lady Margaret Beaufort, passed away on 29 June, just over a week after witnessing the coronation of her grandson Henry VIII. On the same day, James IV confirmed the Treaty of Perpetual Peace and commissioned his most able diplomat, Andrew Forman, Bishop of Moray, to travel to London to meet with Henry and ratify the treaty on his behalf, which was done on 29 August, with all the usual promises of ongoing friendship and peace between the two nations. Around this time, James wrote to Henry and called him his 'dearest brother and cousin', before expressing his thanks for, 'your loving letters written with your own hand, where through we understand the good and kind heart you bear to us, of which we are right glad considering our tenderness of blood.' The two men couldn't help but be suspicious of each other though, despite all these protestations of affection – Henry was well aware that James's nobles were pressuring him to ally himself with the French, while James knew that the hot headed new King of England was no friend to the French and desperate to emulate the military glory of his relative Henry V – a combination that could only end badly.

For now though, they both played the game and hid their true feelings behind florid but ultimately empty declarations of friendship – no doubt much to Margaret's relief. She had been very distressed by the deaths of her father and grandmother, especially as they had come so close together, and her depressed mood was compounded by the fact that she was once again pregnant. It should have been a happy time but after two difficult pregnancies with no children to show for all her suffering, she had no reason to feel optimistic this time around; to soothe her fears, James set out on one of his favourite pilgrimages, to the chapel of Saint Duthac at Tain, where he prayed for a safe delivery and the survival of his wife and their child. Margaret gave birth to another boy, who was named Arthur in honour of her brother, in her chambers at Holyrood Palace on 20 October 1509. Sadly, Margaret's gloomy presentiments turned out to be correct for the baby Prince Arthur lived for only eight months before dying in Edinburgh Castle on 14 July 1510.

Margaret and James were devastated by the death of another child and must have been wondering what was wrong with them. Perhaps the devout

James was even beginning to think that God was punishing him for his part in the death of his father, which no doubt made him even more determined to expiate his sins by leading a crusade to Jerusalem. Even Margaret was starting to wonder if perhaps some divine intervention was called for so, in the spring of 1511, she went on a pilgrimage to the chapel of Saint Duthac at Tain, which her husband had visited so many times in the past. As always, she travelled in style with a huge amount of baggage and every possible comfort, which gave it the appearance of a royal progress rather than an act of faith. Along the way, she visited several of her husband's northern towns and made a state entry into Aberdeen, where she was met on the outskirts by the town burgesses, 'four of whom, attired in velvet robes, carried a crimson canopy over her head, and thus attended her to the gate, where, amid the firing of guns, she was received by a long procession of the inhabitants'. Then, as now, Aberdeen was a lovely city and it welcomed Margaret in style with a decorated procession route and the usual tableaux depicting biblical and historical scenes designed to flatter their royal visitor as well as twenty-four beautiful maidens, dressed in green and wearing white embroidered caps, who played timbrels (tambourines) as they sang a song of welcome to their queen. As usual, the acid-tongued court poet William Dunbar was on hand to record the event for posterity with one of his poems.

> At her coming great was the mirth and joy,
> For at their cross abundantly ran wine;
> Unto her lodging the town did her convey;
> Her for to treat they set their whole ingine.
> A rich present they did to her propine;
> A costly cup that large thing would contain,
> Covered and full of coined gold right fine:
> Be blythe and blissful, burgh of Aberdeen.

It is to be hoped that Margaret found some solace in the serene tranquility of Tain, a place that her husband had been visiting for several years, going there to reflect and gather strength. For his wife, the days of prayer and quiet self reflection were an opportunity to recover from the stress and personal tribulations of the last few years and prepare herself to face whatever was coming next. Although relations between her husband and brother were currently cordial enough it must have been clear, even to someone like Margaret, who had virtually no interest in politics, that it was only a matter of time before the two fell out.

In the meantime, she would soon have something happier to distract her; by the start of August, shortly after her return to Edinburgh, Margaret would discover that she was expecting another baby and thanks to her time at Tain, she was hopeful that this pregnancy would have a happier result. Certainly, she seemed to have rather more energy this time – in October, when she was three months pregnant, she even surprised her husband with a visit while he was staying on the *Great Michael* shortly before it was due to launch. The huge 1,000 ton warship, which was 240 ft long and carried 1,420 men, was one of the wonders of Europe and King James's pride and joy, not least because it made him the envy of other European kings, including his brother-in-law Henry VIII, who immediately countered by ordering an equally massive ship, which was to be known as the Henri Grâce à Dieu. James probably found Henry's adolescent posturing highly amusing but he was much less entertained by the young King of England's next move, which was to join Pope Julius II's new version of the League of Cambrai, his so called 'Holy League', which teamed the Papal States, their old enemy Venice, Spain, the Holy Roman Empire and now England, against France. Henry was thirsting for glory and joining the Papal league gave him a golden opportunity to resume hostilities with the French, whom he perceived to be the natural enemies of England – and with good cause. Naturally he was keen for James to join him but the Scottish king was hesitant to act as he knew that most of his nobles favoured an alliance with France and had also received an urgent request from Louis XII that he renew the Auld Alliance and join forces with the French against their gathering enemies.

As storm clouds gathered, Margaret spent her time preparing for the arrival of her baby and was markedly more devout when it came to her attendance of Mass, no doubt because she still hoped to win God's favour for her pregnancy. Once the winter season at Holyrood Palace was over, she decided to move on to Linlithgow Palace in the spring, having decided to have the baby there instead of at Holyrood. Perhaps she felt that her rooms there had too many sad associations and hoped that a change of scenery would make a difference. While Margaret was preparing to leave for Linlithgow Palace, an official emissary arrived at Holyrood from Pope Julius II bearing a letter outlining Julius's plans to put a permanent end to French oppression in Italy and demanding that James either join his Holy League against this common enemy 'or at least abstain from giving aid to France'.

James was so appalled by the Pope's request that he did not dictate a reply for a fortnight, clearly needing time to calm down and mull over his response, which was very measured considering the agitation he felt. James began by telling the Pope that he read his letter with 'great regret', and went on to ask, 'What can be worse than that a Holy Father and a Christian son should level their swords at each other's throats?' He advised the Pope that he had instructed the Bishop of Moray to urge Louis to reconcile, but his arguments had fallen on deaf ears; James was nonetheless 'resolved to exhort the King of France to return to his obedience; let Bologna be replaced, Ferrara restored and the new Council ceased', believing that he might 'succeed better by peaceful means'. He also reminded the Pope about his plans to lead a holy crusade to Jerusalem, hopefully accompanied by his fellow kings, now peacefully united against a common enemy. James added a postscript in his own hand, asking the Pope to let him know if he wanted him to intervene with the King of France and promising that he 'will try to bring France over, whatever the result may be.' A few days later, James sat down to write to Henry of England and Ferdinand of Aragon, both of whom had asked him to join the Holy League, to beg them now as Catholic kings not to draw their swords against their fellow Catholics and to work with him to bring a peaceful end to the hostilities. He also asked Margaret, an indifferent letter writer at the best of times, to write her own letters of appeal to her brother and his father-in-law, hoping, ultimately in vain, that she might have some personal influence upon them.

By the start of April, Margaret was installed in her magnificent apartments at Linlithgow Palace, where she prayed daily that her child would be healthy and survive. Although the relationship between her husband and brother was tense, Margaret was very pleased to receive from Henry the loan of a special holy relic, the girdle of Our Lady, which was usually housed in Westminster Abbey and said to be especially beneficial to women in labour. Margaret also sent for another relic, the 'sark' (shift) of Saint Margaret of Scotland, who had a special relevance for Margaret as she too had been an English princess who married a Scottish king. On 10 April 1512, Margaret gave birth to another son, who was baptised James in the chapel royal of Linlithgow Palace the following day, Easter Sunday. The new parents were cautiously delighted to welcome their son, but the baby prince was not robust and there was much concern when he failed to thrive on the milk of a number of wet-nurses before a suitable one was eventually found for him.

James celebrated the birth of his son with a lavish banquet at Linlithgow Palace, which seems to have been a rather raucous affair – probably because Margaret, who was once again slow to recover, was not in attendance. She had her chance to celebrate shortly afterwards though when she hosted an extravagant banquet at Holyrood Palace for her brother's special ambassadors Thomas, Lord Dacre, the Warden General of the Marches, and Dr Nicholas West, who would later be made Bishop of Ely. Dacre and West arrived at the Scottish court on 5 May and had been tasked with the job of persuading James to repudiate the French and join the Holy League. For his part, Henry was busily preparing for war with the French, encouraged by his wife Catherine, and there was little chance he would pay any heed to James's attempts to promote peace. There was also little chance that he would pay attention to James's complaints about Henry's deliberate withholding of the bequests that had been made to Margaret by her father, brother Arthur (who had left her all of his possessions), and grandmother Lady Margaret Beaufort, who had left her a collection of valuable jewels.

Over three years had passed since the deaths of Henry VII and his mother and Margaret had still not seen any of the money and goods she had been promised. Other than one polite letter asking her brother when she could expect to receive her grandmother's bequest, Margaret and James had remained silent about the matter, but James had had enough of his brother-in-law's high-handed behaviour and so brought the subject up in his meetings with the English ambassadors, informing them that it was his belief that Henry was withholding the money and jewels in order to spite him. Which was probably accurate, to be fair, although naturally Dacre hastened to deny this, while privately reminding Henry that the 'honourable' course of action would be to hand over his sister's legacy, especially as it was so small.

Although James would no doubt rather have stayed out of the whole affair and instead concentrate on making plans for his crusade, he still felt attached to the Auld Alliance that had existed between his nation and France for generations and so, telling himself that allying himself with King Louis was probably the best way to advocate for peace and get the French monarch to see reason, he agreed to renew the treaty. On 22 May, Louis declared the new version of the alliance, which stipulated that its primary purpose was to provide mutual assistance in the event of hostilities by the English and 'that in the event of war, immediately on receiving notification from Scotland, France shall levy war on England; and *vice versa*'. It also required that no Scotsmen or Frenchmen would be allowed to give aid to the English and that neither nation could make a truce with England without the consent of the other.

James may have had his qualms but he duly signed the agreement in Edinburgh on 20 July, in the presence of several high-ranking churchmen and nobles. The die was cast and now he could only hope and pray that his negotiations with Henry, which were seemingly going quite well, would avert any possibility that he might have to act upon the terms of the treaty and go to war. In the meantime, he wrote to his uncle, King John of Denmark, alerting him to the fact that the English had declared war on France and would almost certainly turn their attentions to Scotland at some point, asking him what help he would be able to provide should King Henry's armies invade. Although, these were worrying times for the Scottish court, James and Margaret still managed to enjoy a lovely summer at Linlithgow Palace and although she had only given birth at the start of April, by June she was pregnant again and with Prince James thriving at last, they no doubt allowed themselves to feel optimistic that this pregnancy would also end happily.

While Margaret prepared for her baby's arrival, she probably had little idea that tensions were rapidly escalating throughout Europe, as evidenced by the endless stream of letters passing between the monarchs of the Pope's Holy League as they prepared for war against France. James was still doing his best to promote peace, as he had promised Pope Julius that he would do, but despite his best efforts, Louis remained obdurate, while his association with the French meant that his brother-in-law Henry was becoming increasingly hostile. By September 1512, plans were being made to send English troops up to the border area in case James decided to attack. Thanks to Henry's excellent network of informants, which he had inherited from his father, he knew that King Louis had been encouraging James to invade England but was of the opinion that as long as the French were not offering any financial incentives to go to war on their behalf, then James would continue to hold off. However, Queen Catherine was in favour of attacking the Scots, justifying her position in a letter to Cardinal Christopher Bainbridge, Archbishop of York, on 18 September with the argument that:

> although the King of Scots promised the King [Henry] to be faithful to England, and swore it to Dr West who was there recently, when he saw that England made war on the French and would send 20,000 men through Normandy under the Earl of Shrewsbury, he began to attack Berwick and denounce war.

It was her belief that James deserved whatever he got for his perfidy and for refusing to join the Holy League with her husband and father; later on she would encourage Bainbridge to put pressure on the Pope to threaten to excommunicate James if he persisted in siding with the French – a terrible punishment for such a devout man, as Catherine must have known.

At the end of November, Margaret prematurely gave birth to a daughter in her chambers at Holyrood Palace but sadly the baby did not thrive and died shortly after being baptised. One of the few mentions of this child in the official records occurred on 10 December when Darcy added a postscript to one of his official letters to King Henry to inform his king that: 'Sir, the Queen's grace, your sister, hath departed with child; it had cristendome and is diseased [deceased]. She is sorry for any grudge between you and her husband.' Margaret was just 23-years-old and had been pregnant five times with only one living child to show for it. She was depressed, exhausted, disappointed and once again failed to rally, which hardly seems surprising in the circumstances. Even the gift of eight rolls of cloth-of-gold from King Louis of France (reported to Henry by the watchful Dacre in the same letter of 10 December as proof that the Scottish and French were in cahoots and plotting an invasion of England) failed to cheer her up, and once again James was so worried about her physical and emotional wellbeing that he made one of his pilgrimages to the chapel of Saint Duthac.

It failed to do the trick though and several months would pass before Margaret felt herself again, although she managed to preside as usual over the court festivities at Holyrood that Christmas before relapsing and taking to her bed in January. The mounting hostilities between her brother and husband can't have helped much as she struggled to recover. Throughout the crisis, James had been sending Andrew Forman, Bishop of Moray, who was one of his most trusted and effective counsellors, on diplomatic missions to England, France and Italy, all with the approval of Henry, who issued him with permits to travel through his territory. However, in the wake of Dacre's letter, this permission was suddenly withheld, enraging James, who saw it for the pointlessly spiteful act that it undoubtedly was.

There was also the matter of the Lord High Admiral of Scotland Sir Andrew Barton, a Scottish privateer with royal permission to seize and plunder Portuguese ships. At the end of the previous year, he and his brother Robert had looted a Portuguese ship off the coast of Kent, not realising that it was carrying goods destined for England. At another time, Henry might well have turned a blind eye, but he was in a vindictive mood and so retaliated by sending two of his own admirals, Sir Edward Howard and his brother Sir Thomas, the eldest sons of the Earl of Surrey, in pursuit. The intrepid popular hero Andrew Barton was killed in the ensuing battle and the survivors captured and imprisoned in London, where it was intended that they should be tried and probably executed for piracy, until Henry relented and let them return home to Scotland.

James was thoroughly infuriated by his brother-in-law's high-handed manner. He turned 39 in March 1512 and had been King of Scotland for almost twenty-four years, whereas Henry would turn 21 in June of that year and had been king for just three years. It seemed incredible to him that this arrogant youngster with comparatively little experience of kingship should presume to square off against him at every opportunity – and that was without going into the relatively parvenu origins of the Tudor family compared to the Stewarts, which made Henry's repeated assertions that James and Scotland owed fealty to him as their overlord almost laughable if they hadn't been so pathetically malicious. Of course, James knew that the root cause of all this bluster, spite and posturing was the fact that until Henry and Catherine produced a living child, something that they had hitherto failed to do, his wife Margaret was heiress to the English throne, and after her would most likely come their son James, who was now thriving in the royal nursery. Still, it was in James's nature to be conciliatory and so he continued his efforts to bring about a peaceful end to the crisis.

In December, he wrote once again to his uncle, King John of Denmark, to announce the birth and death of his most recent child and to complain about Henry's behaviour, writing that he had had no news from England, that his brother-in-law had still not made any proper reparation for the ships lost during Andrew Barton's final battle, and that his own attempts to make peace had been ignored. A few days later he wrote again to the Pope, stressing that he was doing all he could, and deeply regretted that the ridiculous rowing between the Catholic princes of Europe was distracting their attention away from his plans to lead a crusade into the Holy Land.

He wrote again to his uncle on 12 January, complaining that his attempts to promote peace between France and England had not succeeded due to Henry's declaration that he could not make terms with King Louis without the permission of the Pope and his father-in-law Ferdinand of Aragon. He was also frustrated by Henry's refusal to give James's ambassadors safe passage through England, which severely compromised his ability to negotiate with other foreign powers. It seemed to him that despite his best efforts, Henry was so determined to go to war with France that he would not listen to any arguments against it, and was in fact deliberately obstructing James's attempts to negotiate for peace. More worrying though was that Henry had made no secret of the fact he would have to neutralise the threat of Scotland if he went to war with France, and so would invade both countries in order to protect the security of his nation, which would otherwise be left vulnerable to attack from the north.

Indeed, as James reported indignantly to his uncle, Henry had been boasting that he would conquer and ultimately occupy both countries, and had been busily raising taxes in order to fund this great enterprise. James ended this depressing missive by again requesting that his uncle let him have some ships to help strengthen his defence against an English attack – but John died on 20 February 1513 not long after receiving his nephew's letter and was succeeded by his son Christian. Pope Julius II, instigator of the Holy League that had caused all this trouble for James, died the following day having given in to Cardinal Bainbridge's demands that an interdict be placed upon the people of Scotland in punishment for their king breaking his treaty with England in order to ally with the French. Not only that, he also gave Bainbridge the power to excommunicate James himself if he persisted with his fell intent of invading England.

Margaret was still recovering from her illness while all of this was going on so may well have known very little about it as she had never had much of an interest in politics and James probably felt she already had enough to deal with without the burden of a burgeoning war between her brother and husband. By March though she was well enough to receive Dr Nicholas West, who had been sent back to Scotland by Henry, with strict instructions to discover exactly what James was planning, and if possible, to get his plans in writing. It was Holy Week when West arrived at Edinburgh and to his disappointment he was informed that James was spending the whole week sequestered on a spiritual retreat with the Observant Franciscans that he had installed at Stirling Castle and would not be able to meet with him until he had returned to court for the Easter celebrations. He was able to meet with Queen Margaret though, and delivered letters that had been sent up by her family, which pleased her very much and made her exclaim that 'if I were now in my great sickness again then this were enough to make me whole', before adding that she hoped her brother Henry had not abandoned her. West eventually managed to have a word with James two days later, just before the king attended Mass on Easter Sunday and was relieved, bearing in mind the unsatisfactory experience of Thomas Wolsey when he tried to meet with James in 1508, to be welcomed with relative cordiality and invited to speak properly with him the following day. In the meantime he was summoned to dine with Queen Margaret that afternoon, which also went well because his hostess was keen to talk about her brother and, as he reported back to Henry, asked endless questions about him 'especially of your stature and goodly personage'. Henry had been a boy of 12 when Margaret left for Scotland in the summer of 1503 and she must have had many reports since then of his unusual height and good looks – both of which he had inherited from their maternal grandfather Edward IV, who had been a golden-haired giant of a man just like his grandson. She also wanted to know all about Henry's efforts to prepare his navy – perhaps her husband's enthusiasm for his own nascent navy had rubbed off on her, or perhaps she was fishing for information about her brother's plans. After dinner, they sat down together for a chat and West reported back to his master that Margaret was 'right heavy' when he informed her, no doubt not very gently, that her brother was determined to go ahead with his war against France.

She later asked again about her withheld legacy and West, acting on strict instructions from Henry, brusquely told her that she could have the money and jewels as soon as her husband promised not to get involved in the coming conflict. But this James would not promise to do and, three weeks later on 10 April, West left the Scottish court defeated, confused and infuriated by the Scottish king's obstinacy and refusal to comply with English demands. Before he left Scotland he paid one last visit to Margaret at Linlithgow Palace in order to collect letters and presents that she wanted him to give to her brother, sister Mary, and sister-in-law Queen Catherine. She expressed regret that her husband had not been more forthcoming with him then took him to the royal nursery to show him her son Prince James, whose first birthday it was. In the report that he sent ahead to London, West would rather tactlessly inform King Henry, whom everyone in Europe knew was desperate for a male heir of his own, that the boy was 'a right fair child, and large for his age', which no doubt didn't please Henry overly much, especially as this bouncing, healthy Scottish baby was in line to inherit his throne if he didn't manage to produce an heir of his own. Perhaps Margaret was hoping that the sight of her infant son, the personification of the alliance that her father had brokered between the Stewarts and Tudors over a decade earlier, might soften West's heart and make him more favourable to James when he made his report to her brother – not realising that it would take more than her baby's winsome smiles and a few presents to avert the war that they were all inexorably heading towards.

Chapter 11

The Flowers of Scotland 1513–1514

On 11 April 1513, the day after West departed for England, Margaret sat down in her beautiful apartments in the palace of Linlithgow and dictated a letter to her brother in a curious mixture of her native English and the Scots dialect that she had picked up since living in Scotland:

> Right excellent, right high and mighty prince, our dearest and best beloved brother, We commend us unto you in our most hearty wise. Your ambassador, Doctor West, delivered us your loving letter, in which you shew us that where you heard of our sickness [after the birth of her daughter] you took great heaviness. Dearest brother, we are greatly rejoiced that we see you have respect to our disease, and therefore we give you our hearty thanks, and your writing is to us good comfort. We cannot believe that of your mind, or by your command, we are so fremly [poorly] dealt with in our father's legacy, whereof we would not have spoken nor written, had not the Doctor [West] now spoken to us of the same in his credence. Our husband knows it is withholden for his sake, and will recompense us so far as the Doctor shews him. We are ashamed therewith, and would God never word had been thereof. It is not worth such estimation as in your divers letters of the same; and we lack nothing; our husband is ever the longer the better to us, as knows God, who, right high and mighty prince, our dearest and best beloved brother, have you in governance. Given under our signet at our palace of Linlithgow, the xi day of April.

Margaret was clearly very stung both by the withholding of her legacy, which she tactfully suggested could not possibly be Henry's doing but the work of some other malign influence about him, and also some suggestion on Henry's part that she only wanted it because her husband was such a poor king that he was incapable of providing for her. Although Margaret clearly felt herself pulled between the country of her birth and the one that she had adopted after marriage, she obviously wanted to make it plain to her brother that her ultimate loyalty was to her husband. Obviously she would have been much happier if James had gone along with the wishes of her brother and joined the Holy League against France, certainly he would not be facing the interdiction of his nation and excommunication for himself if he had done so, but as he had pointed out to the sceptical West during his visit, he felt himself bound to the French not just by the ancient Auld Alliance between their nations, but also by the fact that Louis, unlike Henry, had promised to help fund James's beloved crusade.

That spring, the French ramped up their campaign to win James's definite support and an agreement that he would invade England should Henry take any aggressive action towards France. Louis offered James all the support necessary for such a campaign – supplies for his troops, armaments for James's ships, 50,000 francs and the loan of his finest and most seasoned admiral, all of which must have been very tempting to James, who had depleted coffers and therefore had no wish to finance an invasion. Louis's wife Anne, Duchess of Brittany, added her pleas and sent James a personal letter begging for his help and asking him to be her champion in exchange for 14,000 crowns. Enclosed with the letter was her glove and a turquoise ring – just the sort of gesture that a chivalrous, romantic man like James found impossible to resist, as Anne and her wily husband Louis must surely have known. Margaret, however, was not impressed by the Queen of France's message and flew into a tearful rage when it became clear that James had been very much moved by it, accusing him of preferring a woman that he had never met to his own wife and child.

Henry was disappointed but not surprised by the failure of West's mission, which marked a quickening towards the inevitable end of the Treaty of Perpetual Peace, and declared that if James had only been more compliant then he, Henry, would have made him Duke of York in recognition of the fact that the next King of England,

> must come either of him or of me, for I have none as yet lawful of my body, but I hear say that Margaret my eldest sister has an heir male of good expectation. I pray God to bless him and keep him from his enemies, and that I may see him in honour and estimation.

At the end of June, Henry departed for Calais with his army, leaving Queen Catherine as regent with the Earl of Surrey in charge of the country's defence against Scotland – much to his displeasure as he would rather have been going to France with everyone else. As soon as news arrived in Scotland that Henry had begun his invasion of France, James prepared to honour his agreement with King Louis and got ready for war. He sent his senior herald, Sir William Comyn of Inverallochy, to France at the end of July, bearing a letter in which he detailed the various crimes that Henry had committed against him, including the withholding of Margaret's legacy and Cardinal Bainbridge's deliberate attempts to ruin his reputation at the Vatican, and formally declaring his intention to ally himself with the French and 'do what he trusts will make Henry abandon his attack on him'. Comyn arrived at Henry's camp on 11 August and was no doubt extremely nervous as he braced himself to deliver his missive and provoke a royal tantrum. He was right to be worried as Henry was predictably furious when he read James's letter and demanded that Comyn take a message back to James that he, Henry, was 'the very owner of Scotland and he holds it through homage to me. Now contrary to his bounders duty as my vassal, he rebels against me. And tell him that with God's help I shall expel him from his kingdom on my return.' The spirited Comyn is said to have replied that he 'may not say such words of reproach to him to whom alone I owe my allegiance and faith', which probably didn't go down well with the English king.

Back in Scotland, James didn't bother waiting for Henry's reply before he began his preparations for war, sending his ships off to join the French royal navy at Brest and mustering his troops. As James no doubt anticipated, anti-English feeling in Scotland was so high that he had no difficulty at all in attracting soldiers from all over the country, all eager to swarm over the border and invade their hated neighbour. The fact that King Henry had declared that he was the rightful owner of Scotland and that their beloved King James was his vassal would only have fuelled their fire even more as this would have been considered an intolerable insult to the proud Scots, who prided themselves on their fierce independence.

As the hour for departure approached, James took himself off on what would be his last ever pilgrimage to his beloved shrine of Saint Duthac at Tain before riding down to Linlithgow, where Margaret was spending the summer with their son. She had just discovered that she was expecting another baby – a piece of bittersweet news at a time when her world was in such turmoil. She begged James not to go, claiming to have had premonitions of his death through terrible dreams in which her jewels turned into pearls, the symbol of mourning, and her husband fell to his death from a great height, but James responded by calmly telling her to go back to sleep. In vain did she remind him that he only had one son, and if he died then baby James would be King of Scotland, but even this did not change James's mind. It must have been a painful parting when the time finally came for him to say goodbye – although there was no real reason to anticipate disaster, Margaret was nonetheless distraught and absolutely convinced that he was going to his death. While James, an experienced warrior, remained outwardly calm and resolute in the face of his wife's tears, he must have felt terrible sorrow and guilt to have been leaving her and his son alone to face their fate. At the very end, she offered to come with him, having heard that her sister-in-law Catherine had accompanied the English army north. 'If we shall meet who knows what God by our means may bring to pass?' James, however, remained adamant that she should stay behind.

While Margaret waited for news at Linlithgow Palace, James and his army, which comprised some 42,000 men, the largest force ever to invade England, advanced towards the border, which they crossed on 22 August before moving on to successfully besiege Norham Castle and then two other castles. Their luck ran out on 9 September though when they finally met with the Earl of Surrey and his army on a field, now known as Flodden field, near Branxton in Northumberland. At first, James had every reason to think that the battle would go his way; after all he had the larger army, around 34,000 men against Surrey's 26,000, but it rapidly began to go awry for the Scots after they charged down their hill towards the English and found themselves dangerously hampered by the waterlogged, muddy state of the field at the bottom. The battle was furious and lasted for just three hours; those fortunate enough to survive and return home would tell bloodcurdling tales of terrible slaughter and bloodshed as the pikes carried by most of the Scottish troops proved no match at all for the more deadly bill, a weapon similar to a halberd, employed by the English, while the Scottish artillery – of which James had been so proud – failed them. By the end of the day, around 12,000 Scots lay dead, among them much of the nobility, the so called 'Flowers of Scotland', which, included four of James's five chief commanders: the Earls of Montrose, Bothwell, Lennox and Argyll, as well as his Lord High Constable, the Earl of Erroll, and his relative, the Earl of Morton, who had welcomed Margaret to his home, Dalkeith Palace, over a decade earlier. Also dead was Alexander Stewart, the king's 20-year-old son by his former mistress Marion Boyd, who had been made Archbishop of Saint Andrews and then Lord Chancellor of Scotland by his adoring father. So terrible were the casualties on the Scottish side that it was said afterwards that every family in Scotland, both high and low, lost someone on that dreadful day, with countless women widowed and their children left without a father. It was a disaster for all of Scotland and it would be some considerable time before the country fully recovered from Flodden.

Survivors would later talk about seeing King James leading the charge against the English and then fighting furiously in the very heart of all the carnage, giving no quarter to the enemy and showing enormous courage until he was hit in the jaw by an arrow, then quickly overcome and killed while fighting his way towards the Earl of Surrey. By the time his body was discovered, it had been stripped naked and was so disfigured as to be virtually unrecognisable. In the end it was Lord Dacre, the Warden General of the Marches, who identified the fallen king's remains – no doubt with a great deal of sorrow, for he had met James, and Margaret, several times and had liked him very much. He would later ruefully note that the Scots 'love me the worst of any Englishman, because I was the one who found the body of their King'. Dacre took the body to Berwick-upon-Tweed, where it was identified by two captured members of James's court before being embalmed and encased in lead and beginning its journey by stages to Sheen Priory, near Richmond Palace. The stages of James's sad last journey – Berwick, Newcastle, York, Sheen, echo in reverse those of Margaret's triumphant progress north just ten years earlier. His bloodstained and torn apart surcoat was sent on ahead to Queen Catherine, who was waiting for news at Woburn Abbey in Bedfordshire, and she immediately sent it on to her husband in France, along with a triumphant letter crowing over their victory:

> My Lord Howard hath sent me a letter, open, to your Grace, within one of mine, by which ye shall see at length the great victory that our Lord hath sent your subjects in your absence... to my thinking, this battle hath been to your Grace and all your realm the greatest honour that could be, and more than you should win all the crown of France; thanked be to God of it, and I am sure your Grace forgetteth not to do this, which shall be cause to send you many more such great victories, as I trust he shall do. My husband, for hastiness, with Rougecross I could not send your Grace the piece of the King of Scots' coat which John Glynn now brings. In this your Grace shall see how I keep my promise, sending you for your banners

106

a King's coat. I thought to send himself unto you, but your Englishmens' hearts would not suffer it. It should have been better for him to have been in peace than have this reward. All that God sends is for the best.

Although Henry was jubilant to hear that his forces had crushed the Scottish forces so decisively, and was relieved to have such a significant threat to his nation's security so efficiently neutralised, he could also be sentimental and had an intense reverence for the sanctity of anointed kingship. He had taunted and insulted James by claiming ownership of Scotland and deriding him as his mere vassal, but in reality he had accepted James as a fellow king, if only for the sake of his sister and therefore the prestige of the wider Tudor family. One gets the sense that it was not just the unnamed 'Englishmen' of Catherine's letter who were dismayed by her original plan to send James's mutilated body to France, but also her husband, who would have been appalled by this offensively cavalier treatment of the remains of an anointed monarch. When he returned to England, Henry would write to Pope Leo in order to request permission to bury James's body with all possible honour in St Paul's Cathedral, London – as the Scottish king had been excommunicated as punishment for breaking his treaty with the English, he had lost the right to be buried in sanctified ground. The Pope duly sent Henry written permission to go ahead with the burial but it never happened and James's body remained at Sheen until the Reformation in the mid 1530s, unburied and mostly forgotten and now, five centuries later, entirely lost to history, its final resting place unmarked and unknown.

Back in Scotland, Margaret waited at Linlithgow Palace for news of her husband and his troops. According to legend, she spent her days in a small bower at the top of one of the palace turrets, which commanded an impressive view across the surrounding countryside. Although she had claimed to have had premonitions of her husband's death in battle, she still hoped that he would return safely to her side. Sadly though, when news of Flodden's tragic outcome arrived in Linlithgow three days after the battle, it was even worse than anyone could have anticipated. Not only was their popular, beloved King James dead, but a significant number of his council and most prominent nobility had perished alongside him.

Only James's Chamberlain, Lord Home, returned from the battle alive, after mounting an unsuccessful attempt to recapture the Scottish artillery, which had been seized as spoils of war by the victorious Surrey. Although Margaret was obviously devastated by the news, she still managed to act swiftly and decisively, immediately removing her toddler son, who was now King of Scotland, from Linlithgow Palace to the superior safety of the almost impregnable Stirling Castle. There, on Wednesday 21 September, less than a fortnight after Flodden, the 17-month-old was crowned James V of Scotland in a ceremony that would later become known as the Mourning Coronation as it is said that the nobles present wept for their dead as the crown was placed on the child king's head by James Beaton, Archbishop of Glasgow.

According to the terms of James IV's final will, Margaret was appointed regent (or as he termed it 'tutrix') for their son during his minority, which was not entirely popular with his remaining nobility. Although Margaret now spoke their language and had taken pains to present herself as a loyal Scottish subject, there were still many who suspected her of remaining loyal to the country of her birth. Anti-English feeling was, understandably, at an all-time high in the wake of Flodden, and the fact that Margaret's brother Henry was regarded as the author of their downfall only fuelled their suspicion of her loyalties and motivations. However, the fact that James had included a clause which ordered that Margaret should be immediately replaced as regent should she remarry gave them some comfort, as it meant there was no chance that Henry, or some other foreign power, might manipulate Scottish affairs by enticing the widowed queen into remarrying one of their own. This had clearly also been James's intention – he was not a spiteful man, quite the reverse in fact, but clearly saw the potential for disaster should his widow pick someone who did not have the best interests of Scotland at heart as her second husband. This was a very real fear – within just a few days of Flodden, the Venetians were discussing whether Margaret might not make a suitable second wife for the widower Emperor Maximilian – a plan that would almost certainly have found favour with her brother Henry. Margaret was not even 24-years-old and, although she was currently preoccupied with grieving for her husband, protecting the interests of her son and preparing for the arrival of another baby, there was still a high chance that she would eventually want to marry again one day – and as mother to the King of Scotland, it was imperative that she chose wisely.

One of Margaret's first actions after the death of her husband was to summon the remaining members of his council to Stirling Castle, where the terms of his will were announced. There was some grumbling about her regency but they all seemed to accept King James's wishes – for now. There were many though that believed that it would have been more appropriate to summon James's cousin, the Duke of Albany, back from France where he had lived all his life, being born there after his father, James IV's uncle Alexander Stewart, fled there in 1479 and married French aristocrat Anne de la Tour d'Auvergne. During the early years of James and Margaret's marriage, Albany had been heir presumptive to the throne, a position that he now occupied again until Margaret's baby was born, and he was apparently ready and willing to step into the role of regent, tacitly backed by Louis XII, who had written to Margaret to express his deep sorrow and distress at the death of King James.

Fully aware of the awkwardness of her position, Margaret turned in vain to her brother Henry, writing to beg him for peace but receiving a dismissive response that made it plain that she was on her own. As always, Henry had his own agenda and it did not involve his sister. Within a week of his victory at Flodden, he wrote to Lord Dacre giving him instructions to do whatever necessary to seize the young King of Scots and bring him to England for he was the 'natural guardian' of his nephew. Dacre was warned not to do anything that might alarm the Scots so much that they moved the young King further away from the border or, more inconveniently, to one of their islands, which would make him more difficult to attain. The only comfort that Margaret was to receive from her family came, rather ironically, from her sister-in-law Queen Catherine, who wrote to express her regret and sent a friar to Margaret in order to give her comfort during her time of sorrow. What Margaret made of this overture is anyone's guess, but it's likely that she was grateful for any kindness from her own family at this point and didn't consider it hypocritical.

For the last ten years, ever since she had first arrived in Scotland as an inexperienced bride of just 13, Margaret had performed her duties as Queen of Scotland to perfection. She had been a magnificently dressed, always well-behaved asset to James's court, presiding over official functions and greeting important visitors. She had also been a good wife – although their marriage was not especially romantic, they were fond of each other and she had done her best to provide James with an heir to his throne, as well as providing him with all the support that he required, even at the end when he was at loggerheads with her brother. She had never taken much interest in politics and indeed had not been encouraged to do so by either her father or husband, which is a shame as any lessons in statecraft that they might have given her would probably have come in useful now, as she found herself suddenly in charge of the governance of a whole nation. Although her husband's council had been depleted by Flodden, she still had thirty-three lords, both temporal and spiritual, available to sit on the general council, with a rota of six councillors specifically tasked with the important job of attending her on a daily basis and vetting any decisions that she might make on her son's behalf. On hand to personally advise and direct her as she took up the reins of government for the first time were the new Chancellor, James Beaton, Archbishop of Glasgow, and a triumvirate of mighty Scottish Earls – Huntly, Home and Angus.

Together, Margaret and her advisors faced the monumental task of uniting a country that had been devastated by the events at Flodden Field, where grief, anger and fear about further English reprisals had led to an outbreak of serious social disorder. Margaret and the council were forced to make two royal proclamations, the first denouncing the looting and molestation of women and children, and the second declaring in the name of the new King James V that all looting, robbery, deflowering of maidens and rape of the widows of Flodden was banned 'on pain of treason'. The situation of women was particularly dire at this time – over 12,000 men, a significant proportion of the Scottish population, had not come home from Flodden Field, which left countless women without male protection and with uncertain futures as they struggled to assert their rights to property and assets, while keeping themselves and their children safe from harm. Margaret did her best for the women of Scotland, but most of her attention was directed towards the defence of the nation as, like everyone else, she was afraid that they were about to be invaded by marauding English troops; it quickly became clear that, for now at least, they were in for nothing worse than a harrying of the border lands in retaliation for the havoc that King James and his men had wreaked on Northumberland on their way south. This was a huge relief because, although plenty of Scots were keen to revenge themselves upon the English for the death of their beloved king, the sad fact was that the army had been severely depleted and demoralised by their defeat and there weren't enough available troops to defend the kingdom against serious attack.

Although there was a growing pro-French contingent who believed that the regency should be given to Albany, Margaret's position was significantly strengthened when the council met at Perth on 26 November and confirmed that there would be no opposition to the terms of King James's will, and that they would support her regency. At the same time they agreed that the alliance between Scotland and France must continue, and that even though there was no plan to make Albany regent, he should still be invited to come to Scotland in order to assist in its defence against the English. Henry was predictably infuriated when he heard that the Scottish council was making overtures to Albany, fearing that this was just the thin end of the wedge and that once Albany was ensconced in Scotland, it was only a matter of time before he had usurped Margaret's power and seized the position of regent for himself.

Henry remained convinced that he was the most appropriate guardian for the young King of Scotland and had no wish to see his nephew in the clutches of the French. However, although his sister tried her best to promote peace between their two nations, Henry continued to prevaricate and did not agree to a truce until February 1514, but it was only to last for a year and a day, and Margaret would have to work hard to get it extended. A more skilled diplomat, such as Margaret's future daughter-in-law Marie de Guise, might have relished the challenging position that she now found herself in, but unfortunately Margaret was in no way equipped to deal with the seemingly endless difficulties that she found herself up against. If she had expected support or sympathy from her brother then she was to be bitterly disappointed, for he either had no understanding of her position – or simply didn't care. Either way, she would have quickly realised that there was no point expecting much assistance from Henry. The fact that the Scottish council and a significant proportion of her people believed her to be loyal to English interests, and her brother's obedient puppet, just added insult to injury because nothing could be further from the truth.

On 14 March, Margaret opened the session of the Scottish Parliament that she had called after her husband was killed. She was eight-months pregnant and despite all the stress and difficulties of her position, she was blooming with health. To the cheering citizens who lined the Royal Mile in Edinburgh, she appeared like a real life Madonna, a fecund symbol of better times to come and a sign that all was not lost for Scotland and her people. Although Margaret must have been exhausted and longing to put her feet up, she behaved graciously throughout the day's ceremonies, giving a speech that recognised the great efforts that her council and the members of Parliament had made to restore equanimity to the nation after the terrible tragedy of the previous year, before leaving the serious business of the day to the Members of Parliament. However, although she had made a good impression upon the people of Edinburgh, the gentlemen of her son's Parliament remained suspicious of their English-born queen and made to seize control of all the main fortresses of Scotland – a provocative move to which she tacitly agreed, but which must have rankled as it demonstrated just how little she was trusted. Margaret's attention was soon diverted elsewhere though; just over six weeks later on 30 April, she gave birth to another son in her chambers at Stirling Castle. The child was given the title Earl of Ross and baptised Alexander, a traditional Scottish royal name that would have recalled to mind the great King Alexander III, as well as her husband's son Alexander Stewart, the young Archbishop of Saint Andrews, who had perished with him at Flodden.

While Margaret recovered from childbirth at Stirling Castle and prepared to be churched at the beginning of summer, her future had become a matter of intense interest to her brother. The death of the French queen, Anne of Brittany, on 9 January had left her husband Louis XII a widower and on the lookout for another wife to provide him with a son because according to French law, his two daughters by Anne would not be able to succeed him. Margaret had been spoken of as a potential bride for the French king right from the start, but the fact that she was still pregnant by her first husband had obviously meant that no formal offer for her hand could be made. Once Prince Alexander had been born though, the match was talked of again; the fact that she had recently given birth to a second son was considered a point in her favour as it proved that not only was she fecund, but also that she had previous form for producing male children. At the same time, there was still some talk that she might make an excellent wife for another grand, but rather off-puttingly elderly widower – Maximilian I, which would be an even more splendid match because it would make her an Empress. However, while her future marital prospects were being discussed in the courts of Europe, and it looked like there was a real chance that she might end up becoming either Queen of France or Holy Roman Empress, Margaret had quietly been making marriage plans of her own.

Chapter 12

A Struggle for Power 1514–1515

Sadly, there is no official record of the occasion when Margaret first set eyes upon Archibald Douglas, who succeeded his grandfather as 6th Earl of Angus in October 1513, but it's likely that she had been vaguely aware of him for much of her time in Scotland before they formed a closer association after the death of her husband. Archibald's grandfather, the 5th Earl had been known at court by the soubriquet 'Bell the Cat', and had managed to make himself one of the most powerful noblemen in the country under James IV, with whom he shared the favours of the beautiful Janet Kennedy (interestingly, Archibald's maternal aunt was Margaret Drummond, who had also been one of James IV's mistresses before being allegedly poisoned with two of her sisters).

The fearsome 5th Earl did not fight at Flodden, but in common with many of his compatriots, he lost two of his sons in the battle, including Archibald's father, George Douglas, who was his heir. Devastated by these losses, the earl went into a decline and passed away within the month, leaving the 24-year-old Archibald to take his place. Handsome, affable and obviously very attractive to women, the new Earl of Angus created quite a stir at court and seems to have quickly attracted the attention of the widowed queen, who was the same age and keen to be distracted from the difficulties of the position she had been left in after her husband's death. What had begun as a discreet flirtation between a widowed young queen and a handsome earl (who had conveniently been widowed himself in 1513 when his first wife Margaret Hepburn, daughter of the Earl of Bothwell, died in childbirth), very quickly took on a more serious flavour though and at some point, either of her own volition or because he had persuaded her into it, she began to consider the possibility of marrying Archibald. Although their union was, on Margaret's side at least, clearly a romantic union, it also seems that she believed, wrongly as it turned out, that her position with her council would be strengthened if she took one of the country's leading peers, a important member of that same council, as her husband. Perhaps Archibald had even managed to persuade her that he was far more popular than he actually was, and that marriage to him would bring her other disaffected and distrustful councillors to heel. Certainly they seemed to be blithely and foolishly optimistic that Margaret would be allowed to continue as regent, despite the terms of her late husband's will which had specified that her regency should be terminated as soon as she married again.

There is also the possibility that Margaret, who was as strong willed as the rest of the Tudor clan, was less than impressed by the various matches that were being considered for her and decided to take matters into her own hands – much as her younger sister Mary would later do when she married Charles Brandon, Duke of Suffolk. At just 24-years-old, the thought of being married off to a much older man such as Emperor Maximilian, or Louis of France, must have been unappealing so it is understandable that she should prefer to marry a man of her own age instead. Her brother Henry's high-handed behaviour over the last few years had undoubtedly rankled as well, and Margaret was not keen to oblige him by becoming a pawn in his attempts to increase his prestige on the European stage. He had already taken one husband away from her – she would not allow him to choose the next. Perhaps tellingly, most of the Tudor state papers and letters of this period seem to be preoccupied with the marital prospects of Margaret's younger sister, Princess Mary, who had been their father's favourite and was said to be the most beautiful, elegant and accomplished princess in all Europe. Mary's betrothal to Catherine of Aragon's nephew, the Archduke Charles, had recently been dissolved and she was now to be married instead to the widowed Louis XII of France, much to the annoyance of the Imperial court. Perhaps it had annoyed Margaret as well – after all, she too had been suggested as a potential bride for the newly widowed King of France and, if Dacre is to be believed, had been ready and willing to become his bride. To be overlooked in favour of her younger sister must have stung, and the fact that Mary was always spoken of as the beauty of the family must have made her feel even worse, so perhaps it is unsurprising that Margaret resolved to, as Jane Austen might have phrased it, marry in order to disoblige her family.

Whatever her motivation might have been, whether it was down to lust, personal pride, pique or misplaced self preservation, Margaret secretly married Archibald on 14 August 1514 in the old parish church of Kinnoull in Perth. Just a few weeks earlier on 12 July she had wowed a convocation of the council at a meeting in Edinburgh, which led them to sign a declaration that they were:

content to stand in one mind and will, and to concur with all the lords of the realm, to the pleasure of our master the king's grace, your grace, and for the common weal; and to use non other hands, now nor in times to come, in the contrary thereof.

In other words, they were willing to put all personal rivalries aside and unite behind her regency, which should have ushered in a period of calm and mutual respect between the widowed queen and council and enabled them to work together relatively peacefully to restore order to the realm. Instead, Margaret threw away the only political advantage she had and completely destroyed her relationship with the council and, by extension, the Scottish people. If Archibald had managed to persuade Margaret that he was popular and influential enough to protect her against the storm their marriage would inevitably provoke, then he had grievously misled her. In actual fact, he was very much in the pocket of his grandfather, Lord Drummond, who had in all likelihood orchestrated the entire affair by persuading Archibald to forget his existing betrothal to the beautiful Lady Jane Stewart, sister of the Laird of Traquair, and instead pursue the king's mother. The Drummonds were not a popular clan and the Douglas family were even more disliked in Scotland thanks to their vainglorious, back-stabbing and scheming behaviour. Despite her apparent lack of interest in politics either at home or abroad, Margaret must still surely have caught some wind of the general loathing of the Douglas family at court, which makes her decision to marry Archibald, already a huge error of judgement, even more reprehensible.

The council were quick to move against the newlyweds, demanding that Margaret appear before them to defend her decision before informing her that, according to the terms of her first husband's will, she had forfeited her right to act as regent for her son and that they had already decided that the Duke of Albany should be invited to come to Scotland and take over the reins of government. As they put it in their official declaration:

We have shown heretofore our willingness to honour the queen contrary to the ancient law and custom of this kingdom. We have suffered and obeyed her authority the whiles she herself kept her right by keeping her widowhood. Now she has quit it by marrying, why should we not choose another to succeed in the place she has voluntarily left?

The only question that remained was whether Margaret would also be required to give up custody of her sons. When the council sent the herald Sir William Comyn to Margaret a few weeks later to inform her that they had met at Dunfermline on 21 September and almost unanimously voted to remove her from her position, he found himself in the unpleasant position of being confronted by an angry Archibald, along with a hostile coterie of his disgruntled relatives. The council's demand that Margaret's new husband should appear before them in order to explain himself was scornfully rejected, but it was when Comyn unwisely referred to Margaret not as 'the Queen's grace', but instead as the much less prestigious 'My Lady the King's mother' (a reflection of the fact that she was no longer Queen of Scotland but instead merely the Countess of Angus), that all hell broke loose. Archibald's fearsome uncle, Lord Drummond stepped forward and struck the unfortunate herald across the face – although even this assault was probably much less terrifying than Comyn's last important task, which was to take James IV's declaration of war to Henry VIII in France.

Margaret was doubtless apprehensive about her brother's reaction to her news and was probably relieved when Henry, usually so quick to express his disapproval and extremely miserly when it came to dispensing praise or congratulations, had very little to say about the matter other than to urge his sister to resist the Scottish council's attempts to replace her with the Duke of Albany, who was more French than Scottish and could therefore potentially be hostile to English interests. What he said in private about his sister's choice of second husband and resulting struggle to retain power in Scotland is anyone's guess but it is not likely to have been very kind.

When the council voted that Margaret had forfeited the office of regent and tutrix (guardian) of her son, they also decided that letters should be sent with all haste to the Duke of Albany, requesting him to return as soon as possible to take her place. To add insult to injury, they informed Margaret that they would require her agreement to do so 'with the consent of her husband'. Naturally, the newly married pair had no wish to comply with this request, but Margaret at least quickly realised that she had little choice in the matter and so grudgingly gave her consent. As Albany was happily installed at the French court and had shown no apparent desire to ever return to Scotland, it's likely that she was hoping he would refuse to come, plus there was the promise that Louis XII had made to her not to send Albany unless she herself requested his assistance, which had been reiterated when he married her youngest sister Mary.

Nonetheless, she must have waited with bated breath for his response to the summons taken to him by the intrepid Sir William Comyn, who at least could be assured that for once he would be greeted with some pleasure. His assault by Lord Drummond had only served to increase the enmity that already existed between the council and Douglas faction, although Margaret would later half-heartedly do her best to downplay the incident by claiming that her husband's uncle had not struck Comyn but rather 'wafted his sleeve' at him before pushing his chest. The damage was already done though and the incident was chalked up as yet another example of why she needed to be removed from a position of influence.

In retaliation for this and other incidents of poor behaviour on the part of Archibald, who physically attacked the Lord Chancellor in order to seize control of the Great Seal, and his relatives, they ceased all payments of Margaret's jointure, which was drawn from the dower lands that had been agreed at the time of her marriage to James IV. This left her in dire need of money because Archibald, although wealthy, was certainly not equipped to keep her in the manner to which she had become accustomed during her ten pampered years as Queen of Scotland. He was putting pressure on her to have his uncle, Gavin Douglas, nominated as Archbishop of Saint Andrews, a position that traditionally came with guardianship of the king and a huge income drawn from the vast and wealthy diocese of Saint Andrews. However, this went directly against the wishes of both the council, whose nominee was James Hepburn, and Pope Leo X, who favoured Andrew Forman, the Bishop of Moray, who had been so busy on James IV's behalf during the crisis that ultimately led to Flodden.

The already volatile situation quickly descended into violence as the great clans seized this opportunity to show their disapproval of the Douglas family, and at the end of October, the furious Hepburns and Lord Fleming joined forces to lay siege to Saint Andrews Castle, trapping Gavin Douglas inside. Margaret sent Archibald away from the safety of Stirling Castle to help his uncle then, on 22 November, sat down to write a lengthy letter to her brother Henry, informing him that her 'party adversary continues in their malice and proceeds in their Parliament, usurping the King's authority, as I and my lords were of no reputation, reputing us as rebels; wherefore I beseech you that you would make haste with your army, both by sea and land'. This was treasonous talk and if the letter, which was to be conveyed to Henry via Lord Dacre, had been intercepted it might well have landed Margaret in even worse trouble than she was already in. 'I am at great expenses,' Margaret went on to complain, 'every day a thousand in wages, and my money is near hand wasted; if you send not the sooner other succours of men or money, I shall be super expended, which were to my dishonour.' She then turned to the thorny subject of Albany, who was still in France:

> All the hope that my party adversary hath is in the Duke of Albany's coming, which I beseech you to hinder in any way; for if he happen to come before your army, I doubt that some of my party will incline to him for dread. I shall keep this castle with my children till I hear from you. There are some lords that dread that your army shall do them scathe, and that their lands shall be destroyed with the fury of the army; wherefore I would that you wrote to them that their lands nor goods shall not be hurt, and, if so be, that they shall be recompensed double and treble.

After asking for Henry's assistance in the matter of the Archbishopric of Saint Andrews, she concluded with a request that he should:

> direct writings to me each month, at the least, how you will do, and what you would that I did; and if my party adversary counterfeit any letters in my name, or if they compel me to write to you for concord, the subscription shall be but thus – Margaret R and no more, and trust that such writing is not my will. Brother, all the welfare of me and my children lies in your hands, which I pray Jesus to help and keep eternally to his pleasure.

Clearly she was afraid that her letters would either be intercepted, forged or coerced from her, which shows just how poor and mutually distrustful relations were between Margaret and her son's council – probably for very good reason. The deadly impasse between them was reflected by the violence and strife that was erupting throughout the country, which led Dacre, safe on the borders but with spies everywhere, to write to her brother Henry's council in London that 'there was never so much lawlessness in Scotland as now'. It seemed as though the country, so briefly united in sorrow by the death of their king just a year earlier, was now on the brink of civil war.

The English troops that Margaret expected to appear at any minute to rescue her from her predicament never materialised. Although Henry had originally promised her military assistance, he was now worried that any meddling in Scottish affairs would adversely affect the good relationship that he was currently enjoying with France, now that his youngest sister Mary was queen there. The fact that Margaret's intended replacement as regent was half French, had lived in France all his life and was favoured by Mary's husband Louis XII was also a complication that Henry could do without. When King Louis died on 1 January 1515, 18-year-old Mary was left isolated at the French court, especially as, unlike her sister Margaret, she had no royal child to use as a bargaining chip in any ensuing struggle for power. The French throne was inherited by Louis' 20-year-old cousin and son-in-law François, Duc d'Angoulême, who behaved with great courtesy towards Mary and appeared open to continuing the friendship that her marriage had established between his kingdom and England. However, he was also sympathetic to the pleas of the Scottish council and encouraged Albany, who as predicted was not keen to leave his comfortable home in France, to consider accepting the regency of James V.

Henry, never the most doting of brothers, was nonetheless sufficiently alarmed by the vulnerability of Mary's position in France to continue to exercise restraint when it came to the crisis in Scotland, fearing that any wrong move might have unfortunate repercussions for his youngest sister. When Henry's best friend Charles Brandon, Duke of Suffolk, was despatched to France at the end of January to bring Mary home, he was also given the task of doing whatever he could to prevent the Duke of Albany from leaving for Scotland by reminding the new King François of his predecessor's promise not to send Albany to Scotland unless Margaret herself requested it. At the same time, Henry put pressure on the Pope to agree to the promotion of his sister's uncle-in-law, Gavin Douglas, to the Archbishopric of Saint Andrews and wrote to Margaret (who was disappointed not to have been rescued by an English army), to urge her to escape to England, bringing her two sons with her, after which he would do all that he could to support her cause.

By this time, Henry and Catherine had lost four pregnancies, the most recently when she gave birth to a stillborn baby boy that winter, and rumours were beginning to swirl around the courts of Europe that he was looking for ways to extricate himself from his marriage. Whether the rumours were true or not, it seems that publicly at least, Henry was trying to put a brave face on the matter and behaving as though he had accepted that he and Catherine, whom he still loved very dearly, might not be blessed with a child of their own. If this was indeed to be the case, then the sons of his sister Margaret would be next in line to the throne and to her surprise he now proposed making the eldest boy, James, heir to the English throne, while the younger, Alexander, would inherit Scotland.

Margaret wrote back to let Henry know that although she would be glad to leave Scotland and thought she might easily be able to get away if she disguised herself, she did not think it would be possible to bring the two boys with her and that there was no great need for haste because she did not believe any of them were in personal danger. She was also extremely loath to remove the little king from his country, fearing that to do so might result in him being deposed from his throne. She also must have known that it would do him no good to be raised in an enemy court – as far as the Scots were concerned, the English had stolen their last king away from them and it was very unlikely that they would stomach losing another.

The council had actually told Margaret that she was welcome to retain custody of her two sons if she would relinquish the regency but, no doubt encouraged by Archibald and his family, she had haughtily refused to do so. Now, she piteously informed her brother that: 'God send I were such a woman as might go with my bairns in my arms, then I promise I would not be long from you.' She was not such a woman though, she was an anointed queen and as such believed that her duty was to remain in Scotland – she did not fear for her life but told her brother that she was afraid her current state of poverty might make her more amenable than she might otherwise have been to the council's demands because she had no means to defend herself against them. In the meantime, she remained shut up in Stirling Castle with Archibald and her sons, declaring that there was no one she could truly trust but her husband and his uncle and ignoring Dacre's pleas that she put her trust in him and let him convey her across the border into England.

At the beginning of March, the news arrived in England that Princess Mary, the dowager Queen of France had secretly married the Duke of Suffolk with the connivance of King François. It is likely that she felt emboldened by her elder sister Margaret's second marriage to a man of her choice and, with all the airy confidence of youth, was wilfully disregarding the trouble that this alliance had landed her in. Henry must have felt singularly put upon as he dealt with the consequences of both of his sisters' marital escapades, especially as Mary was insisting that he had given his permission to let her choose her second husband herself.

At the same time as Henry was coming to terms with the marriage of his youngest sister and his best friend, the mischievous King François was arranging for the Duke of Albany to make his long anticipated journey to Scotland. Ahead of him went a letter from François to the council, in which he assured them of his wish to continue the Auld Alliance between France and Scotland – not least because of the great sacrifice that James IV had made for France – and that they could rely on French assistance and support if they found themselves at war with England. For Margaret, the most alarming part of this missive was the last point, where he stated he had asked the Duke of Albany to make arrangements for her younger son, Prince Alexander, to be raised at the French court. Albany himself left France on 2 April, arriving in Scotland with eight ships full of provisions and 1,000 French soldiers on 18 May, despite last ditch attempts by the Duke of Suffolk to prevent his departure by going to King François and offering him a renewed treaty with England on condition that Albany was kept in France.

Suffolk was also approached by a sea captain who claimed to know the exact route that Albany would take – valuable information if, as was rightly rumoured, Henry was planning to intercept the duke on his way north. Within minutes of landing, Albany had managed to mortally offend Lord Home, who had previously been one of Margaret's most outspoken opponents but had now switched to her side, by making a Latin joke that Home did not understand and therefore decided was deliberately intended to make him look stupid. His reception in Edinburgh went much better though as Margaret graciously gave him the use of her own apartments in Holyrood Palace and removed herself and her household to Edinburgh Castle. Their first meeting went very well – Margaret appeared in great state, determined to remind Albany that she was still an anointed queen, and spoke to him in French, which impressed him a great deal, while Albany charmed her with a level of intellectual conversation that had been in short supply at the Scottish court since her husband was killed. He had also made a very favourable impression upon her sister Mary and her husband the Duke of Suffolk in Paris, both of whom believed that he would deal kindly and fairly with Margaret, and would no doubt have been able to relay messages from them to her.

An urbane, cultivated, intelligent man, Albany was determined to bring order and effective governance to the beleaguered Scots, but knew from the start that if he was to have any chance of success, he would need to have the little king and his baby brother in his care. Albany probably didn't relish the prospect of separating Margaret from her sons, but he did not allow his personal distaste for the task ahead of him deter him from what he strongly believed to be his duty. Although he spoke little English and even less Scots, Albany was still able to easily make friends within the council and when they summoned Margaret to one of their meetings shortly after his arrival, she was stunned and most displeased to find out just how closely they were working together and how little support she had, especially when it came to her children. The councillors nodded in agreement as Albany outlined his plan for the two boys, who would no longer be under Margaret's care but instead raised by four guardians, who would be selected by Albany out of eight candidates presented by the council. Margaret was invited to vet Albany's choices but must have known that this was merely a courtesy and that her feelings on the matter were actually of very little consequence.

The matter was raised again on 12 July when the Scottish Parliament met in Edinburgh. The ceremony began with Albany's formal investiture as regent of Scotland, during which he was handed the sceptre and sword of state before having a coronet placed on his head by the Duke of Argyll and, insultingly, Margaret's husband Archibald. Margaret's brother Henry and Lord Dacre were busily doing their best to undermine Albany's reputation in Scotland by exploiting existing feuds between the clans and 'torment arguments between Albany and Angus and between Albany and the Chamberlain [the Bishop of Glasgow] so as to drive the duke out of Scotland', but with marked failure, although they had some success when his attempts to punish Lord Drummond for striking the herald Sir William Comyn were strongly opposed and eventually resulted in Drummond being pardoned, although he still lost his lands to the crown.

Margaret spent the early summer of 1515 in a state of increasing panic, terrified she was about to lose her children and feeling progressively more helpless in the face of Albany and the council. Although her brother was doing what he could for her, she still felt that he was not doing enough to help and believed all her problems could be easily solved if he would only send an English army over the border. Meanwhile her marriage with Archibald, the root cause of all her issues, was rapidly coming apart at the seams as the couple rowed constantly. Sadly for Margaret, at around the same time as she realised that she could never rely on her husband for support, she also discovered that she was expecting his child and so the summer months were further complicated by the sickness and exhaustion that she suffered during all of her pregnancies.

Nonetheless, she stood her ground with enormous courage when the four guardians selected by Albany came in procession up the hill to Stirling Castle in order to take custody of the boys and return to Edinburgh with them. As the procession of grim-faced men reached the castle entrance, they paused, expecting Margaret, who was holding the boy King James V by the hand while a nurse behind her held the baby Prince Alexander in her arms, to step towards them. Instead she demanded to know why they had come and when they responded that they had come by order of Parliament for the king and his brother, she ordered the castle portcullis to be dropped in their faces. The people of Stirling cheered wildly as the queen, magnificently dressed as always, stepped forward and reminded them that Stirling Castle belonged to her as 'by the late King, my husband, I was made sole governess' – as had by extension the two small boys that the council were planning to wrest away from her. Reminding the people of Stirling that she was the widow of their beloved martyred king was also a masterstroke for it painted Albany, the council and Parliament in a very poor light with the populace, who were already inclined to be sympathetic towards Margaret. She asked the council for six-days grace then turned on her heel and vanished into the castle precincts, followed by her entire household.

Archibald now showed his true colours as he urged Margaret to acquiesce and hand her sons over to Albany. Even Archibald's uncle, Gavin Douglas, for whom he and Margaret had risked so much when they tried to make him Archbishop of Saint Andrews, dismissed his nephew as a 'young witless fool' – and so he proved to be in the face of this latest crisis. While Margaret remained sequestered in her apartments at Stirling Castle, distressed and apprehensive about the future, Archibald slipped out of the castle and headed instead for his own ancestral lands, leaving his younger brother George Douglas to act as Margaret's chief advisor in his absence. As they had anticipated, Albany did not waste time before informing Margaret that he was coming to Stirling himself, whereupon she, in a desperate attempt to keep her children, sent him a message begging to keep the boys so long as she promised to remain in Scotland and if that wasn't acceptable, then she would consider allowing them to pass into the guardianship of her husband, Lord Home, Sir Robert Lauder and Lord Keith, who was Earl Marshal. This, Albany would obviously not agree to and he once again reiterated Parliament's order that the boys should be handed over. In the report he sent to King Henry's council, Lord Dacre wrote that it was his belief that the two boys were doomed if they fell into Albany's hands for there was nothing to stop the duke murdering them both and usurping the Scottish throne for himself – a warning that was intended to remind Henry and his council of the alleged criminal activities of the last Plantagenet king, Richard III. It was Dacre's belief that Henry should write to King François and ask him to intervene with Albany, for the Scottish regent was still a French subject and should therefore do his bidding.

Dacre, who had tried so hard to persuade Margaret to flee Scotland with her children, could only listen helplessly to increasingly alarming reports from Stirling, where Albany, who had not yet arrived but was daily expected, had declared all who remained in the castle to be traitors and publicly stated his intention to starve Margaret out, even asking for her husband's help in cutting the supply lines. Spirited as always, Margaret let it be known that if Albany used any force against her, she would 'set the young King upon the walls in the sight of all persons, crowned, and the sceptre in his hand, so that it shall be manifestly known to every person that the war shall be made against the King's own person.' On 4 August, Albany arrived in person at the gates of Stirling Castle, bringing with him most of the temporal lords and a fearsome force of 7,000 men. More terrifying still though were the cannons that accompanied them, including the enormous Mons Meg, the star of the Scottish artillery, which was capable of firing a 150kg gunstone for over two miles and could easily decimate the walls of Stirling Castle. The terrified George Douglas abandoned Margaret and rode off to join his brother, leaving his beleaguered sister-in-law to face Albany on her own. Margaret knew when she was beaten and immediately surrendered, although she saved some face by making her son, King James, hand the keys to Stirling Castle over to the victorious regent.

Margaret pleaded with Albany to treat her, her sons and her husband with mercy but to her alarm, although Albany agreed that she and her sons would be treated with the greatest kindness and courtesy, he could not promise to behave the same way towards Archibald and other traitors. Within a few days, the boys had been removed from Margaret's care while she was taken back to Edinburgh Castle as a virtual prisoner. Although Albany had promised to treat her well, Margaret clearly saw matters differently for she complained of the rough way that he had deposed her from the throne after he 'came into my Castle of Stirling accompanied by great processions of people having with him also great guns', and of the 'crafty and subtle ways' by which he had overthrown her, taken her own lands away and seized her children. On 20 August 1515, also apparently against her will, she signed a statement that gave her consent to Albany's custody of her children and declared that she agreed he should 'have charge and keeping of the King and his brother'. It was over.

Chapter 13

A Homecoming 1515–1517

In England, news of Margaret's plight was greeted with great indignation, to the extent that the French Ambassador requested leave to return home for he feared violent consequences to Albany's actions. Although the Scottish regent was possibly the most hated man in England at that point, there was no doubt in anyone's minds that he had acted as King François's creature throughout the whole affair and that blame for Margaret's tragic situation rested entirely on the shoulders of the new French king. Towards the end of August, King Henry himself wrote to François to remind him that it was thanks to him that Albany was in Scotland and had usurped his sister's throne and that if any harm should come to Margaret or her sons, he would consider François entirely to blame. However, he also wrote a scathing letter to Margaret, informing her that she was not entirely blameless in the matter and ought to bear some responsibility for the calamities that had befallen both her and her husband's family, who were now being punished by Albany. This did not go down well with his sister, but she managed to reply cordially enough with an assurance that she would do everything possible to maintain peace with the regent. At the same time, Dacre was encouraging her to leave Scotland, writing that she should, 'without further delay think of the high minded and pleasure of the King, my master, your brother. With all the politic ways and wisdom you can use and with all haste possible withdraw yourself from Edinburgh.' Now that she no longer had custody of her children, Margaret felt like there was nothing left to lose and so let it be known to Dacre that she was planning her escape from Albany's clutches. At the same time, Lord Home, who had been involved in a failed plot to kidnap the king and his brother, wrote to Dacre to inform him that not only had Albany forced Margaret to sign her children away to him, but he was also compelling her, against her will, to tell her brother that she was content with her situation, when in fact she was frightened and felt she was being treated with great cruelty by Albany. At the end of his letter he added an ominous postscript informing Dacre that it was 'now or never' to act on Margaret's behalf.

At the start of September, Margaret received permission from Albany to make her way to Linlithgow Palace, her favourite residence. Her baby was due in the middle of October and she let it be known that she was having her apartments there prepared for giving birth. Shortly before setting out, she wrote to Dacre to tell him that this was part of a ruse to facilitate her escape from Scotland and that she was planning to feign illness as soon as she arrived at Linlithgow on 11 September. She would then ask that Archibald be allowed to visit her, after which they would wait two days before slipping away in the dead of night, accompanied only by a handful of faithful retainers.

Dacre had become increasingly important to Margaret over the difficult last twelve months, not least because he acted as conduit for her correspondence with her brother, which passed through his hands. Now, he felt great relief that Margaret was finally about to take his advice and leave Scotland, perhaps for good. It would have been preferable if she had been able to bring her sons with her, but just Margaret alone was better than nothing as far as her brother was concerned. When one considers Margaret's run of poor luck, it was probably a happy surprise to everyone involved when her escape attempt went as planned. She and Angus met with the faithful Lord Home just outside Linlithgow, then rode through the night to the Douglas stronghold of Tantallon Castle. Hearing that Albany was already moving to intercept them, they left the following day, leaving in such haste that most of Margaret's clothes and jewels had to be left behind, and took refuge in Blackadder Castle. The fugitives had barely any time to rest there before they heard that Albany was again hot on their trail and had raised a huge army with which to lay siege to the castle. Fearing imminent capture, Margaret, Archibald and their small entourage rode with all haste across the border, aiming for Berwick-upon-Tweed, where she had been so royally entertained during her last few days on English soil.

Now she was back in England again for the first time in over a decade and presented a sorry contrast to the pampered, beautifully dressed and gracious young Tudor princess she had been before her marriage. To Margaret's great chagrin, she was refused entry to Berwick Castle by the recently appointed new Captain, Sir Anthony Ughtred (who would later marry one of Jane Seymour's sisters); he had received strict orders not to admit anyone who came from Scotland without safe conduct papers. Not even the threats of the always short-tempered Archibald could move him and so in the end the exhausted, mud-splattered little group was forced to turn their horses around and take shelter in Coldstream Priory, which stood on the banks of the Tweed and was very close to Flodden field.

Disappointed to have lost Margaret, Albany immediately focused on damage limitation, fully aware that he would be judged by every court in Europe for having apparently treated her so abominably that she was forced, heavily pregnant and penniless, to escape in the dead of night and leave the country. He did not go himself, but instead sent an emissary, the French Ambassador Monsieur du Plains, to Coldstream with an offer that he thought might tempt the queen to return to Scotland – increased access to her sons, the return of the clothes and jewels that she had left behind, and the restoration of much of her jointure. Unfortunately for him, Lord Dacre arrived in Coldstream first, full of apologies and bearing the necessary travel permits that would allow Margaret to cross the border and take refuge in England. Her husband Archibald, however, was not granted permission to leave Scotland and so the couple were forced to say goodbye, probably not all that unwillingly on Angus's side, before Margaret and the extremely relieved Dacre left for his stronghold, Morpeth Castle.

They had not gone very far though before Margaret, who was close to her due date and completely exhausted by her recent escapades, began to feel labour pains and told her escort that she could not ride much further. Very much alarmed, Dacre immediately changed course for the closer Harbottle Castle, which was smaller and less comfortable than Morpeth but serviceable enough for an emergency stop and unscheduled royal birth. As soon as they arrived, Margaret had to be taken straight to bed and it was there, on 7 October, that she gave birth to a daughter, who would be christened Margaret in the castle chapel the following day with the absent Cardinal Wolsey as godfather. As always, Margaret struggled terribly with labour and once again there was serious concern that she might not survive afterwards, her fever and exhaustion doubtless exacerbated by her recent travails.

Although she was desperately ill after the birth, Margaret rallied enough to be able to write a letter to Albany on 10 October:

> Cousin, I heartily commend me unto you, and where I have been enforced for fear and danger of my life to depart forth of the realm of Scotland, so it is that, by the grace of almighty God, I am now delivered and have a Christian soul, being a young lady.

She then went on to request yet again that she be reinstated as regent and have her sons returned to her custody – by now she would have been well aware that Albany's treatment of her was being reviled throughout Europe and it's likely that Dacre was encouraging her to put pressure on the duke to save face by restoring her to her former position. They were probably not surprised when Albany's response was an unequivocal refusal and a reminder that she had ceased to be queen when her first husband died and then 'forfeited the tutelage of her children' as a result of her second marriage, and that if she did not listen to reason, he would be forced to take sterner measures to prevent the breakdown in relations between England and Scotland that she was trying to promote.

His letter to her sister Mary, who had written to enquire about the health of her nephews and to plead for her sister, was much more friendly, and assured her that he had done Margaret no harm and would do her whatever service he could. Nonetheless, despite the harsh tone of his original letter, Albany soon afterwards sent a messenger offering her the return of her jointure money and the custody of her children if she would only return to Scotland either before her baby was born (obviously it was too late for that), or within eight days of her churching. He begged her to make the decision on her own rather than listening to the advice of those, and by this he meant Dacre, who wished only to create trouble between England and Scotland. Margaret was tempted by this offer, but could not forgive or forget the way she had been treated, and was mistrustful of Albany and his motives, so she opted instead to put her trust in her brother and the efforts of her husband, who was plotting with a group of other powerful Scottish noblemen to kidnap the young king and his brother and have Margaret restored to the regency with him at her side.

Dacre in the meantime was in a state of panic about the condition of Harbottle Castle, which was in need of repair and not at all suitable to act as the residence of an anointed queen and her baby. He and his wife had prepared Morpeth Castle for Margaret's lying-in and he was keen to have her moved there as soon as possible, which of course was frustrated by her continuing poor health after the birth. It was not until 18 October that he wrote to his master King Henry about the sudden arrival of his sister and the subsequent birth of her daughter, whom he described as a 'fair young lady', who had been christened 'with all such convenient provisions as could or might be had in this barren and wild country'. After filling Henry in on all the current activity in Scotland, he finished his letter by stating his intention to move Margaret and her baby to his main residence of Morpeth as soon as possible for it was becoming expensive to keep them at Harbottle.

As Margaret was unwell and suffering great discomfort from sciatica, the result of long hours in the saddle while heavily pregnant, she was unwilling to move any time soon, so the harassed Dacre added that perhaps Henry might 'signify your mind and pleasure unto her, that we may move her accordingly'. This Henry did, in a letter entrusted to one of his favourite gentlemen ushers, Sir Christopher Garneys, who had been despatched up north with all haste to take a cartload of gifts, including twenty-two magnificent fur-trimmed gowns, undergarments, shifts and accessories, plus everything necessary for the layette of a royal princess as well as bed-hangings, plate and furniture. After depositing this booty at Morpeth Castle, Garneys rode on to Harbottle thirty miles away, where Henry's letter was received with much pleasure by his ailing sister; Margaret was very touched to be invited south to join Henry's court for the Christmas festivities that she had always enjoyed before her marriage.

Sadly though this happy family reunion had to be postponed for Margaret was not well enough to leave Harbottle until 26 November, and even then it was clear that she would be unable to go no further than Morpeth. As it was quite impossible for her to ride there, Margaret and her baby travelled by litter with two stops along the way at Cartington Castle and then Brinkburn Priory, finally arriving at Morpeth Castle on 2 December. A few days later she was reunited with her husband, Lord Home and other loyal friends, her brother having given permission for them to visit her.

Henry was keen that his sister should be treated with all possible deference, and ordered that all the dignitaries of Northumberland should pay their respects to Margaret. More pleasing still were the lavish gifts her brother had sent to her with Garneys. On 8 December, Margaret was carried out of her bedchamber in a chair in order to view them, which she did with great pleasure. She was not yet well enough to get dressed up and so was forced to make her servants parade the lovely dresses, particularly one of cloth-of-gold, and another of gold tissue, in front of her several times a day so that she could admire them. Even her male Scottish guests were not spared a viewing of Margaret's new clothes and she showed the dresses off to them, exclaiming: 'Here you can see that my brother the King has not forgotten me, and that he will not let me die for lack of clothes.'

As the royal account books can attest, Margaret had always had a taste for expensive finery, but it had taken on a special significance in recent months as she fought to assert her status in Scotland. As a Tudor she knew the importance of appearing royal at all times in order to underline one's prestige and right to rule, and it had hurt Margaret's pride to be seen without all of her usual fabulous gowns and jewels. Now that relatively friendly lines had been opened with Albany, she sent to Edinburgh for some favourite dresses, with Christopher Garneys, who was rather taken aback by her obsessing over her dress collection, writing to her brother that, 'she is going to have in all haste a gown of purple velvet lined with cloth-of-gold, a gown of right crimson velvet furred with ermine, three gowns more, and three kirtles of satin.'

In December a friendly letter arrived from Henry, regretting her absence at the court's Christmas celebrations and reiterating that she would be most welcome in London and could even bring her husband if she liked. The Dacres were determined that their royal guest would not miss out on all the seasonal festivities though, and spent a great deal of money ensuring that their Christmas celebrations were extremely lavish, with Christopher Garneys reporting to the king that he had never seen a Baron's house better trimmed in all his life with:

> all the hangings of the hall and chambers with the newest device of tapestry, and with all other manner of things thereunto belonging, his cupboard all of gilt plate, with a great cup of fine gold with the cup of assay, and all the lord's board, with the board's end served all with silver vessels, lacking no manner of good victual and wild fowl to put in them, that can be gotten for money.

His description of Margaret, whom he clearly pitied a great deal, was much less happy though, and he wrote that he thought,

> her one of the lowest brought ladies with her great pain of sickness, that I have seen and scape. Her grace hath such a pain in her right leg that this three weeks she may not endure to sit up while her bed is a-making, and when her grace is removed it would pity any man's heart to hear the shrieks and cries that her grace giveth.

Worse was to come though, for Garneys ended the same letter with the ominous lines:

> Dacre must have written of the death of the Prince of Scots. Fears if it came to her knowledge it would be fatal to her, for

these four or five days of her own mind it hath pleased her to show unto me how goodly a child her younger son is, and her grace praiseth him more than she doth the King her eldest son.

Margaret's younger son, Alexander, Duke of Ross, had died suddenly at Stirling Castle on 18 December of an unknown childhood illness. The news arrived at Morpeth at the end of December but Dacre judged Margaret too weak and emotionally vulnerable to deal with the news and so he withheld it from her until March, when she was gently informed that her son was dead. As expected, she took it badly and immediately began to blame Albany for the boy's death, as did her brother. Henry, who was cynically using the situation in Scotland as an excuse to resume hostilities with France, had spent the last few months complaining loudly about Albany's treatment of his sister, accusing him of wilfully usurping her position, stealing her jewels and goods, evicting her from her home and behaving so badly that she felt she had no other option but to flee Scotland in fear of her life.

Albany and his French supporters claimed in vain that Margaret had been treated very well and would not have felt compelled to run away if it weren't for the lies of her husband's family and Lord Dacre, both of whom had used her to further their own agendas. The apparently sudden death of the little prince only served to add fuel to all the accusations about Albany, especially as Dacre and Henry had long been making veiled hints about the crimes of Richard III, who had allegedly murdered his nephews after usurping the throne, and now it seemed to some that they had been proved right and that Albany had allowed his overweening ambition to make him a cold-hearted murderer. As speculation increased that King Henry was on the verge of avenging his sister by declaring war on France, King François tried his best to distance himself from Albany and suggested that he return Margaret's money and goods, pardon her husband and other supporters, return her son to her custody and restore her to her throne. At the same time, Albany was trying to correspond with Cardinal Wolsey to persuade him that he had done nothing wrong in his treatment of Margaret, that it was all just a misunderstanding and he was ready and willing to come to terms with her should she agree to return home to Scotland.

Margaret had continued to ail throughout the beginning of 1516, giving great concern to her hosts, Lord and Lady Dacre. In the middle of January, they asked King Henry to send one of his own doctors up to Morpeth to look at Margaret's leg, for her sciatica seemed to be getting much worse and she was still not able to walk very much. They were also worried about her appetite because she was eating very little, despite Lady Dacre's best efforts to order food that would tempt her as well as the usual invalid foods such as 'almond milk, good broths, pottages and boiled meats'. The main concern though was Margaret's emotional state, for she was obviously very depressed and apprehensive about the future – no wonder therefore that Dacre had decided to withhold the news of her son's death until she was considered better equipped to cope with it. As the months went by though, she began to recover and by the end of March was feeling able to make the long journey south to London. As the crisis between England, France and Scotland escalated, it had become increasingly imperative that she show herself at her brother's court so that she could speak for herself.

Before leaving Morpeth, she wrote to Albany to reiterate her grievances against him, demanding that he release Gavin Douglas and Lord Drummond, who had been imprisoned, and return her husband's castles of Tantallon and Bothwell, as well as the jewels she had left behind in Scotland. She also helped Lord Dacre and Thomas Magnus, one of Henry's chaplains and Archdeacon of East Riding, to put together a lengthy document detailing all of Albany's 'crimes' against her. Margaret's contribution was eight pages of accusations and grievances against the regent, including the death of her son Alexander, signed off in her own hand. However, while Margaret and Henry were working to blacken Albany's name throughout Europe, her husband Archibald was itching to negotiate with the regent and suddenly announced that he would not be accompanying Margaret to London after all, but would instead be returning to Scotland with Lord Home in order to ask for his confiscated lands to be returned. Margaret was desperately hurt by his sudden departure, taking it 'right heavily', and 'making great moan and lamentation', while Dacre was outraged and intercepted the two errant Scottish noblemen at Etall Castle, where he tried in vain to shame them into returning to Margaret's side. The fact of the matter was that Archibald had been corresponding with Albany for quite some time and was already half in his pocket – he would be restored to favour as soon as he arrived at the Scottish court, much to Margaret's disgust, while her brother, whose opinion of Scotland and its people could hardly get any lower, sardonically remarked that Archibald's betrayal was 'done like a Scot'.

Margaret left Morpeth on 8 April and travelled with her baby in a litter sent up by her brother. Dacre, no doubt relieved to be rid of his troublesome royal guests for a while, accompanied them to Newcastle, where they were greeted by the city mayor and Queen Catherine's equerry Sir Thomas Parr (whose daughter Catherine, the future sixth wife of Margaret's brother, had been born in 1512) and then on to Durham, where he took his leave of Margaret and returned home, leaving her in the care of the Earl of Northumberland, who was rather less dashing now than he had been thirteen years earlier when he had delighted Margaret and her ladies with his fancy clothes and riding tricks.

At York, the party was joined by Archibald, who had been despatched as an emissary by his new friend Albany and begged Margaret for permission to join her, but she was still furious about his abandonment a few weeks earlier and refused to let him accompany her to London. By 27 April, Margaret had reached Stony Stratford in Buckinghamshire and wrote a note of thanks to her brother, informing him that, 'so being comforted of you in my journey in many and sundry ways that, loving be to our Lord God, I am in right good health, and as joyous of my said journey toward you as any woman may be in coming to her brother', adding that she was 'most desirous now to come to your presence and to have a sight of your person'.

The next stage of her journey took her to Enfield, where she stayed at the Lord Treasurer's palatial house Elsing Hall for a few days before continuing on to London on 3 May. Impatient and curious to see his sister, Henry rode out and met her at Sir William Compton's mansion, Bruce Castle in Tottenham, eight miles outside the city, bringing with him a whole host of courtiers and a beautiful white palfrey, which was a gift from his wife. Henry then accompanied Margaret and her daughter back to London before leaving her to enjoy the excitement of a state entry to the city where she had been born. Riding her new white palfrey and wearing one of her gorgeous new gowns, Margaret was greeted by cheering crowds as she made her way along Cheapside to Baynard's Castle, the former residence of her grandmother, Lady Margaret Beaufort. She stayed there for four days, recuperating from her long journey south, before travelling down the Thames to Greenwich Palace for a long awaited reunion with her family.

Henry had been 12-years-old and Mary just 7 when Margaret left for Scotland thirteen years earlier, so she must have been astonished by how much they had changed since she had last set eyes upon them. Now in his mid-twenties, Henry was in his prime and still blessed with the athletic physique and golden good looks that made him renowned as one of the most handsome princes in Christendom; the 20-year-old Mary was at the very peak of her beauty and obviously delighted to finally be married to Charles Brandon, whom she had loved for quite some time. Also present was Henry's wife, Queen Catherine, who was heading towards 30 and although still handsome, not quite the lovely Spanish princess who had captured so many hearts at her wedding to Prince Arthur. Any possible awkwardness about their meeting was dispelled by the warmth of Catherine's welcome, but it's not hard to imagine that Margaret might have had misgivings about being in the company of the woman who had sent the army that killed King James at Flodden, and then afterwards gleefully sent his bloody jacket to her husband.

After three failed attempts to provide Henry with an heir, Catherine had finally presented him with a daughter, Mary, that February, their first child to survive for longer than fifty-two days, and she was radiant with happiness that summer as her daughter continued to thrive. Margaret's 6-month-old daughter would join her little cousin in the royal nurseries at Richmond during her visit, while her mother enjoyed the lavish jousts, feasts and entertainments that Henry had organised for her entertainment, including a banquet held in Queen Catherine's apartments and a two-day joust in Margaret's honour, during which her brother and his gentlemen wore purple velvet, embellished with gold roses. It seems likely that at some point, in the midst of all these celebrations, Margaret slipped away to nearby Sheen Priory to visit the resting place of James IV, whose embalmed remains still lay there awaiting the grand funeral that Henry had planned for him, but which would never actually happen.

Exhausted, depressed and stressed after an increasingly difficult few years, Margaret was much revived by the warm welcome she received from her family, and immensely gratified to finally be treated like a queen. Assured of her brother's affection and support, she felt much more able to plan for the future and became even more determined to fight for the restoration of her regency and the return of her son, King James. When they left Greenwich, Margaret and her daughter settled at Scotland Yard, which was traditionally the residence of the Kings of Scotland on the rare occasions they visited London, and a short walk away from Westminster Palace, where she was born and Westminster Abbey, where her parents were buried, although their beautiful tomb was not yet completed. Unlike her brother's dazzling palaces on the Thames, Scotland Yard was rather dilapidated but still comfortable, and Margaret and her daughter lived there happily for the next eleven months, enjoying the central location and the lovely gardens that extended to the riverbank. After spending so many years cut off from her family and feeling isolated at the Scottish court, it must have been a real pleasure to be able to spend time with Mary and Catherine, especially as they both had babies as well – Mary's son Henry Brandon had been born on 11 March and she would soon be pregnant again. Although both Mary and Margaret had taken commoners as their second husbands, they were still referred to as queens and treated as such at court. Although Henry was disappointed that he could no longer use them as collateral by arranging dynastic marriages for them, it still greatly added to his own prestige and cachet on the European stage to have not one but three queens of different kingdoms at his court, even if both of his sisters were embarrassingly short of money and not living in the most regal manner.

Ambassadors sent by Albany had arrived in London before Margaret, but Henry had refused to see them straight away and kept them waiting until he had spoken to his sister and read the document listing her grievances. He finally summoned them to his presence at the end of May and made it clear how displeased he was with Albany's treatment of Margaret – a point he reiterated on 1 June in a very strongly worded letter to the Scottish Parliament, in which he expressed his concern about his nephew King James's safety, and demanded that Albany resign the regency and leave Scotland. The already uneasy treaty between England and Scotland was due to expire on Saint Andrew's Day in November 1516 and Henry requested that the matter be settled before then so that 'further direction may be taken for the common weal of the two kingdoms'. As he must have expected, Albany remained firmly entrenched in Scotland, but his ambassadors continued to meet with Henry for several months, making regular reports back to Edinburgh. Although Margaret could hardly have felt very optimistic about the results of these meetings, she would be pleasantly surprised when their discussions with her brother resulted in Albany and the council giving in to pressure and agreeing to restore her income.

By now she was owed £14,334 – a very handsome sum – but only £114 arrived and by the end of the year, despite some gifts of money from her brother, Margaret was forced to apply to Cardinal Wolsey for a loan of £200 so she could support herself and buy the lavish gifts that were traditionally exchanged at court on New Year's Day. More happily though, they also negotiated for the return of her magnificent jewels, clothes and other chattels that had been left behind, and to her great relief, everything was exactly as she remembered. Anticipating her concerns that her belongings might have been looted or stripped of valuable precious stones, the council furnished her with a full inventory, which makes for fascinating reading today as it gives a splendid insight into the possessions of a sixteenth-century queen. Even though Scotland was a relatively poor country, Margaret still owned piles of gold chains, a huge diamond presented to her by Louis XII, gold collars decorated with enamelled white and red roses, hoods trimmed with precious stones and a beautiful ruby that she wore attached to a black velvet cap, as well as other expensive and dazzling goods. Like many people, she had evidently dealt with low moods and boredom by spending money like water – which was fine when she had the full use of her income, but not possible in her current predicament.

Wolsey was still keen to bring about a marriage between Margaret and the Emperor Maximilian and there were rumours that he was planning to have her marriage annulled on the grounds that it had taken place while Scotland was still under a papal interdict. However, although Archibald was proving to be a less-than-satisfactory husband, Margaret still felt some loyalty towards him and would not consider ending her marriage. There was also the fact that their daughter would be rendered illegitimate if such a course was taken, which was not something that Margaret was prepared to do. She and her daughter spent that Christmas at Greenwich with the rest of their family, participating in the revelries arranged by Henry for the festival.

The grandest took place at epiphany, when there was a grand entertainment called the 'Garden of Esperance' in the great hall, where the guests were thrilled by the appearance of a wheeled set which was decorated to look like a beautiful garden with silk flowers and green satin leaves, among which walked six handsome knights and six lovely ladies, who descended to perform a dance before the royal party. Afterwards, the royal party led their guests into a sumptuous banquet. For Margaret, this was a delicious taste of how life should be, and while it made her miss her life as Queen of Scotland, it also made her more determined to be restored to her previous position. At the start of 1517, she began to make plans to return home, having been assured by Albany that she would be most welcome to come back, but could not expect to be restored to her former position, although she would have all of her funds returned to her. In the middle of April, a travel permit arrived from Scotland and, although she was not confident about the sort of welcome that she would receive (especially from her son, whom she feared would be kept away from her), she had Henry's assurance that he would do all he could to support her cause, even if it brought him into conflict with France. On 18 May, just over a year after she arrived, Margaret took her leave of her family at Windsor Castle and set off for Scotland, laden with gifts which included new 'white damask cloth-of-gold, crimson cloth-of-gold and black velvet' trappings for her horses, gold plate, jewels and new livery. As usual she travelled in easy stages, receiving a great welcome at each town and city that she stopped at along the way. Her brother was a popular king and the people were pleased to see his sister, who was in turn delighted to be treated with such respect. Although her health was much improved, she fell ill at Doncaster and had to rest there for longer than anticipated but was soon on the move again, arriving in York at the beginning of June. It was there that she received the completely unexpected, but very welcome news that Albany had returned to France.

Chapter 14

A Poor Suitor 1517–1523

On 15 June 1517, Margaret and her daughter crossed the border into Scotland. Although Albany's departure had made her more optimistic about the future, she had a last minute change of heart when she reached Berwick-upon-Tweed and considered turning back to London until Lord Dacre arrived and persuaded her to carry on. Once again she was met at Lamberton Kirk, although her reception was rather less grand than the one that had greeted her when she first came to Scotland as a young bride fourteen years earlier. This time she was met by a smaller group, headed by her husband Archibald and his cousin James Douglas, 3rd Earl Morton, who was married to Catherine Stewart, one of James IV's children by Marion Boyd and the younger sister of Alexander Stewart, who had died beside his father at Flodden. Although Archibald had not seen his wife and small daughter for over a year, he had been in no great hurry to greet them and in the end, the council, who were keen to appease Margaret as much as possible, had forced him to go. Also present was Antoine d'Arces, Sieur de la Bastie-sur-Meylan, a French diplomat who was Albany's right-hand-man and had been made Deputy Governor during his absence. He had first met Margaret in the immediate wake of Flodden, when he was despatched by Louis XII to commiserate with the grieving young widow and assure her of French support, and she was doubtless pleased to see him among the company for he had always treated her with great courtesy and kindness – even if he was less than complementary about her in his despatches. Accompanied by an escort of 3,000 soldiers, the company rode on to Edinburgh, where she was to be once again lodged in her old apartments in Holyrood Palace.

Although the council were full of promises about restoring her income, allowing her to retain possession of Stirling Castle and treating her with greater respect, Margaret was to find they were still going to be difficult about enabling her to have contact with her son. As soon as she arrived in Edinburgh, she hurried to the Castle, where he resided under the guardianship of the Earls of Arran, Angus and Argyll and the Archbishops of Glasgow and Saint Andrews, but was refused entry by the governor Sir Patrick Crichton, who kept a stringent control over all comings and goings at the Castle and had not received official permission for Margaret to be allowed access to her son. Although she pleaded with the council to be allowed to see him, she was not permitted to visit James until August, after he had been moved outside Edinburgh to Craigmillar Castle following an outbreak of plague in the capital.

James V turned 6 in April 1518 and was a handsome, serious little boy with the auburn hair and good looks of both of his parents, and Margaret had every reason to be proud of him. He was powerless to do anything to help her though as she continued to battle with the council; eventually she decided to cut her losses and move to Newark Castle, perhaps the least grand of her various jointure properties, but certainly the most economical to run. Despite the promises of Albany and the council, she had seen very little of her income and it would soon become clear to her that they had been diverted all along by her husband, who was living in fine style with his mistress Jane Stewart, to whom he had been betrothed before he was persuaded into courting Margaret's favour. To his wife's indignation, she discovered that not only had this been going on the whole time she was in England, but that they had been openly living together in one of her properties and enjoying a lavish lifestyle, while she had barely enough money to pay her servants. Whatever residual affection Margaret might have had for Archibald vanished completely when she made these terrible discoveries, and she almost certainly began to wish she had been more amenable to Wolsey's proposal to annul her marriage and arrange a more prestigious one for her.

In the past she could perhaps have counted on the support of Lord Home during this difficult time, but Albany had given orders for him to be executed for treason while she was in England. Here, once again, Albany underestimated the fierce loyalties of the Scottish clansmen and within a few months of his departure, his deputy governor, Antoine de la Bastie, had been ambushed and savagely murdered by kinsmen of Lord Home, who then hammered his head to the market cross in the borders town of Duns before crossing the border to seek the protection of Lord Dacre.

His replacement, James Hamilton, 1st Earl of Arran, who was next in line for the throne after the heir presumptive Albany, suspected that Archibald and his family were the real culprits and immediately imprisoned Archibald's hapless younger brother George – starting a bitter and bloody clan war between their families which would last for several years. In the meantime, no doubt thinking he had had a lucky escape, Albany wrote to Margaret and encouraged her to take over the regency. Thinking her position would be strengthened with her husband at her side, she asked the council if they would consider letting her share the regency with Archibald, but they declined the offer, making it clear they preferred to deal with Arran. Margaret's relationship with the council continued to decline over the next few months and by March 1518 she was appealing to Dacre for help, prompting him to appraise Wolsey of her dire situation; she was so poor that she had been forced to pawn the plate that Henry had given her upon her departure from England. The only consolation was that Dacre had been sufficiently wary of Archibald's motives that he had forced him to sign a document renouncing his right to claim her rents on her behalf, but this hadn't stopped him from continuing to take the valuable rents from Methven and Ettrick Forest, and now Margaret's situation was precarious.

In June, Dacre wrote again to Wolsey, reiterating Margaret's woes and describing her as living in Edinburgh with her daughter 'like a poor suitor'. While she herself wrote to her brother that:

> The cause that I came hither most for was for the King my son's sake, and I am holden from him like a stranger, and not like his mother, which doth me great displeasure in my heart, considering I have no other comfort here but him. Therefore, since they will not let me be with my son, nor is not answered of my living, neither to the King my brother's honour nor mine, I beseech his grace to let me come to be in his realm.

Little wonder then that her thoughts were increasingly turning towards ridding herself of Archibald permanently. In October she wrote a pitiful letter to her brother, telling him that:

> I am sore troubled with my Lord of Angus since my last coming to Scotland, and every day more and more, so that we have not been together this half year... I am so minded that, an I may by law of God and to my honour, part with him, for I know well he loves me not, as he shows me daily.

And reiterating her request to be allowed to return to England, writing: 'I beseech your grace to help me, and to give me license to come to your realm.' She closed her letter with a final plea: 'Wherefore, I beseech your grace ... to be a kind prince and brother to me; for I shall never marry but where you will bid me, nor never to part from your grace, for I will never with my will abide into Scotland.' Henry was appalled by her letter and responded that there could be no question of a divorce and that it was her duty to remain in Scotland. Even Margaret's promise to let him choose her next husband did nothing to soften her brother's annoyance and within a few weeks, he had despatched one of his wife's favourite priests, Friar Bonaventure Langley, up to Scotland to try to persuade his errant sister to reconcile with her husband; when he failed, he was replaced by Friar Chadworth, who was also unsuccessful in the face of Margaret's unwavering and understandable loathing of her adulterous, thieving husband.

Disappointed by her blood relatives, Margaret turned to the new deputy, Arran, for help, perhaps encouraged by the fact that his family, the Hamiltons were mortal enemies of her husband's clan. He had previously been able to assist her with getting hold of some of her revenues, although he had only been able to claw back £2,000 rather than the full £9,000 that she was owed, and his demand that Archibald and his mistress leave Margaret's property, Newark Castle (which they had moved into as soon as she vacated it), had fallen on deaf ears, for they were still living the high life with her money. They would have had even more out of her if Archibald's attempts to have the bond he had signed for Dacre cancelled had been successful, as this would have given him the power to seize all of her money and leave her with literally nothing. However Margaret was adamant and won the day - making enemies of Archibald's family, who naturally supported him to the hilt, with the result that she found herself even more isolated in Scotland.

Spurred on by his hatred of the Douglas family, Arran was very active on Margaret's behalf at the beginning of 1519 and helped her to score a point against her husband when he assisted her to make a deal with the council, whereby she exchanged the lands she owned at Ettrick for an annual income of £2,000. As Archibald had been misappropriating the funds from Ettrick for quite some time now, he was furious and staged a protest, reminding the council that he was 'spouse and husband to the Queen's grace, by reason thereof he is lord of her person, dowry and all other goods pertaining to her highness, and may dispose thereupon at his pleasure'. To Margaret's delight, the council, who were as fed up with him as she was, ignored him and she won the day – although as usual she would see very little of the promised money, and Archibald would continue to press his claim for the rents to be restored to him.

At this point, it must have seemed that Margaret's hatred for Archibald would never end, but then she appeared to have a sudden change of heart and wrote to him from Stirling Castle suggesting a rapprochement – a ruse to use him to get what she wanted, but the credit for this spectacular about-face was laid tactfully at the door of the latest persuasive friar sent up to her by Henry and Catherine. Arran, who had done his best to support Margaret and bring her over to the pro-French faction, was appalled and begged her to reconsider throwing her lot in with her faithless husband once again, but she was adamant and, on 15 October, she and Archibald, accompanied by 400 men, rode into Edinburgh and took control of the capital. In public the reconciled couple appeared triumphant, but in private their bitter quarrels continued as Archibald made it plain that he had no intention of giving up his mistress, who had recently borne him another daughter, and continued to misappropriate Margaret's money and possessions. By the end of the year their already uneasy truce was almost at an end and when Margaret fell desperately ill with smallpox that winter, he was probably not the only one hoping she would die and bring the whole affair to a convenient end. Luckily for her, Margaret soon rallied and by the end of summer 1520 she was back on her feet, had repudiated Archibald again, and was back in the Arran camp. Even more surprisingly, she had become so assimilated into the pro-French camp, thanks to the disappointing behaviour of her family, that she was adding her voice to those asking Albany to return to Scotland. The duke, however, was not keen to return and was heard saying he wished he had broken both of his legs before he had ever set foot there.

In the summer of 1520, all of Europe was preoccupied with the long-awaited grand meeting between Henry of England and François of France, which took place near Calais in June. As one of the highest-ranking nobles at François's court, Albany was expected to attend and while there he had the opportunity to talk with Henry and Wolsey in person about Margaret's situation. François was all in favour of his return to Scotland but Henry, who had no wish to see the French getting a foothold in Scotland again, did not agree with his sister that Albany was the best hope for the embattled nation and persuaded the French king to keep the duke in France. He had been corresponding with his brother-in-law Archibald, who was just the sort of superficially charming, flashy and athletic young man that Henry tended to admire, and come to the conclusion that a joint regency of Margaret and her husband was the best way to promote English interests in Scotland and keep the meddling French out of the country.

Unfortunately, his sister's loathing of her husband was a serious hindrance to Henry's plans, and when another letter detailing her woes arrived while he was in France, he could barely hide his impatience with her. François remained sympathetic to Margaret though, and the memorandum prepared before their meeting lists the arrangements that he was prepared to make for her in return for her agreement to have Albany back: free visitation rights to her son and the return of all of her property. However, Henry was uninterested in discussing Albany's return to Scotland and so François despatched the duke to Rome instead, where he could begin discreetly working to bring about Margaret's divorce, gaining close proximity to Pope Leo X thanks to the fact that his recently deceased sister-in-law, Madeleine de la Tour d'Auvergne, had been married to the Pope's nephew, Lorenzo II de'Medici (the couple's daughter Caterina is better known as Catherine de' Medici and would later marry King François' son, Henri).

Margaret's truculent mood was not improved by the barrage of letters that now came her way from England, especially from her devout sister-in-law Catherine, who was appalled that Margaret was talking about divorcing Archibald. Dacre also wrote and infuriated Margaret by asking her to remember her obligations to her family, and making it clear that if Margaret continued to side with Arran, Albany and the pro-French faction in Scotland, she would be effectively estranging herself from her family, for they would no longer be able to support her. His pleas and threats fell on deaf ears – Margaret continued to write to Albany, who was working on her behalf in Rome and even sent her money, which was more than her brother had done. In the spring of 1521, Margaret replied in her own hand to Dacre's most recent letter, which urged her once again to return to her husband, by curtly pointing out that if Archibald 'had desired my company or my love, he would have shown him more kindly than he hath done', and then reminding him of the dreadful way her husband had treated her since her return to Scotland. She ended on a bitter note, saying: 'I had no help of his Grace my brother, nor no love of my lord of Angus and he to take my living at his pleasure and despoil'. She would have been even more disturbed if she'd known that Dacre and Wolsey, desperate to prevent the French from using Margaret to gain a foothold in Scotland, were colluding with her husband and his family to spread rumours that she and Albany were more than just political allies and that they were planning to marry as soon as she had secured her divorce.

Margaret was jubilant when Albany arrived back in Scotland on 18 November 1521 and rushed to welcome him at Stirling Castle, the scene of their stand off in 1515 and now backdrop to their reconciliation. They entered Edinburgh together a few days later, where they called upon her son and, to Margaret's immense gratification, Albany presented her with the castle keys, signifying that from now on she would be free to visit her son whenever she liked, just as he had promised.

Within days of returning, Albany had seized all power from the hands of the Douglas family, expelling them from the high positions they had been placed in, and charged Archibald and his uncle Gavin Douglas, Bishop of Dunkeld, with high treason. Both men immediately made for the borders then separated, with Archibald seeking the protection of Albany's great enemy Lord Dacre, while Gavin made his way down to London to spill their woes at Henry's feet. He also added his voice to the rumours that Margaret and Albany were lovers and plotting to do away with anyone who stood in their way, and that Albany was mistreating the young king and enriching his own coffers while making Margaret and her children live in poverty. They were incensed when they heard that Dacre was probably harbouring the fugitive Archibald and wrote stern letters to him, reminding him of the truce that existed between their countries. Albany was more tactful and said that he did not believe Henry could have any knowledge of what Dacre was up to, but Margaret was more forthright and accused him of deliberately causing trouble between herself and her brother, and now taking her estranged husband's side against her. Dacre's response was to accuse Albany of having told her what to write, then deny all of their charges against him before reminding Margaret that she had married Archibald without the permission of her brother and, whatever his faults, she must now make the best of things.

Although Wolsey, Dacre and her brother were keen to undermine Albany in every possible way, and did their best to persuade Margaret that he was just using her for his own ends, Margaret completely ignored them. Thanks to the duke, she was being treated better than she had been for quite a few years and she felt she had every reason to be grateful to him; if her brother really cared about her, he ought to be grateful to Albany also for restoring her to her position, reuniting her with her son, and significantly improving her financial situation. She was deeply distressed, therefore, when Henry, who had until now been letting his displeasure be known to her via Dacre, sent the Clarencieux Herald, Thomas Benolt, north with letters for Margaret, Albany and the Scottish Parliament, and an additional scathing verbal message for his sister that made his annoyance plain. The letters openly accused the pair of all the perfidy that the Douglas faction had been spreading about them since Archibald and his uncle were expelled from Scotland; Margaret was appalled and astounded that her brother gave even the slightest credence to the story that she was having an affair with Albany and planning to marry him once he'd managed to secure her divorce. Henry's letter to Albany was, if anything, even more offensive – charging the duke, whom he must have known was utterly devoted to his French wife, with deliberately seducing Margaret in order to get his hands on her sons, and also 'the dishonourable and damnable abusing of our sister, inciting and stirring her to be divorced from her lawful husband for what corrupt intent God knows.'

More seriously, he once again asserted his legally and morally dubious authority over Scotland and accused Albany of returning there without his permission before demanding that he leave immediately, or 'face the brunt of battle'. Albany could hardly believe his eyes as he read the letter and swore on the Holy Sacrament to Benolt that he had never had any intention of either seducing or marrying Margaret as he had 'enough with one wife'. He added that he greatly marvelled that 'the King's Highness, upon light reports, would have the queen his sister to be so openly slandered – as if I kept the said queen as if she were my wife or my concubine.' Luckily for Albany, Henry's letter to Parliament was greeted with the same incredulity and the members had no hesitation in informing the English king that they had complete confidence in the Duke and no intention of removing him from his position.

Margaret was wounded by her brother's behaviour. It seemed that she had spent her whole life being loyal to her family, and it hurt her very much to be turned on now – especially as it was clear from his letter and message that Henry not only sided with her abusive, thieving husband, but was also apparently willing to listen to the slanderous tales being spread by the Douglases, Dacre and Wolsey. In the circumstances, her reply was remarkably measured, although there was more than a hint of steel in her words when she wrote:

> I think it will not be to your honour to suffer such false and untrue report made upon me, your sister. It had been your part, dearest brother, to have been my defender in all evil reports, and not to have alleged wrongously dishonour to me; which shall prove of the self, false and contrary.

She then reminded him that:

> I was constrained to make me friends, through my good bearing toward my Lord Governor of Scotland, wherein I have

> found me more kindness not I have in any other in these parts.
> Suppose that your grace be pleased that I say this, I may say as
> I find cause hitherto; and if I did find the contrary, I should say
> it. But your grace may do to me, your sister, as ye please, but
> I shall make no evil cause, but it does me great displeasure in
> my heart of your unkindness.

She went on to inform her brother that contrary to what he had heard from Archibald's 'wicked' uncle Gavin, her son James was very well cared for and indeed flourishing, and there was no truth at all to stories that he was being mistreated by Albany. For good measure, Margaret added that if Henry did not desist from attempting to meddle in her son's upbringing then 'the world will think that he aims for his nephew's destruction'. It was no secret that Henry believed James would be better off with him, but Margaret made it plain that she did not believe such an arrangement would be to her son's benefit – for even if Henry did not mean to do him actual harm, he would still ruin James's chances of earning the trust and affection of his people, who had no great love for their English neighbours.

At the same time as Margaret was protesting her innocence, Albany was corresponding with King François, who was trying to persuade him to invade England. In November 1522, the uneasy truce between François and Henry had finally fallen apart when Margaret's brother joined forces with the Papacy and the Holy Roman Empire, which was now ruled by Emperor Charles V, against the French. Another English invasion of northern France seemed inevitable and so François naturally turned to their old allies, the Scots, for help. Albany, always more loyal to the French than the Scottish, was happy to help – but he was no fool and knew that the memory of Flodden and its bitter aftermath still loomed large in Scotland; he would have a very hard time persuading the council and Parliament to take the English on again. When he eventually managed to muster a large army, Margaret reacted with alarm and moved her son out of harm's way to the virtually impregnable Stirling Castle before begging both the duke, who made it as far as Carlisle, and Dacre, whose job was to defend the border region against Scottish hostilities, to come to terms before all was lost. As nobody had any great appetite for war, she had no difficulty brokering a peace deal and even rode out to Berwick herself to oversee the signing of the treaty. Having been denied any true authority for a long time, it pleased Margaret to be in the position of making peace between England and Scotland and she no doubt hoped that her brother would see the gesture as proof that she was still as loyal as ever to the country of her birth.

Although Henry was not best pleased that a treaty had been agreed without his input, he was indeed relieved to be spared a war with the Scots while he was preoccupied once more with fighting the French. King François however was not at all happy with Albany, whom he had ordered to invade the English, and the duke was immediately recalled to France. Margaret was disappointed to lose Albany, who promised to return with more French troops and money by the following August, but Henry was jubilant. No doubt Archibald would also have been pleased, but he had been captured in the borders several months earlier by Albany's men and forcibly exiled to France, where he would remain, effectively neutralised, for the foreseeable future.

If Margaret felt alarmed to lose Albany's protection, she was no doubt mollified to find herself back in her brother's favour now that the duke was gone. Seizing this opportunity to sever Margaret from the pro-French party at the Scottish court, Henry offered his sister a five-year truce, money and a marriage between his daughter Mary and her son James if she would only agree to prevent Albany from returning, and repudiate the Auld Alliance between Scotland and France. Although Margaret felt more comfortable siding with the English, her only concern was the security and wellbeing of her son; although she wanted to be able to trust her brother, she could not forget how he abandoned her when she had needed him most, nor how easy and pleasant her life had been during Albany's second regency. She corresponded with both sides throughout 1523, never fully repudiating the French, but at the same time not throwing her lot in with the English either. Meanwhile, the Earl of Surrey, son of the earl who had escorted Margaret to Scotland before her first marriage, had been made Lieutenant General of the Marches and been despatched to harry the Scottish borders, where he was gleefully ordering raids and savagely attacking the towns and villages on the Scottish side – including Kelso, which was virtually razed to the ground. Margaret was dismayed by this brutality and wrote to Surrey, begging him to behave less roughly, and even to spare her friends, such as the Prioress of Coldstream; when she discovered that the prioress had been complaining about her however, she quickly changed her tune and ordered Surrey to set fire to the convent.

To Margaret's mind, there was no point harassing the already impoverished peasants and farmers who lived in the borders when making a decisive strike at Edinburgh, which was not much further away, would have a greater impact. She was also thinking about ways the current situation could be used to benefit her son and it seemed to her that if the country was weakened by English hostilities, there would be little resistance to the coup she had been considering for some time and which would, she hoped, place her son more firmly on the throne – with herself as the power behind it.

Chapter 15

Beset on all Sides 1523–1529

Margaret's adored only son, James V, turned 11 in April 1523. A bright, handsome, charming and intelligent boy, he was enormously popular and considered by many to be a worthy successor to his father. It was widely believed that once James reached his majority on his fourteenth birthday, he would be a king that the Scottish people could be proud of. Encouraged by Surrey, who believed that James's emancipation was the easiest route to dispelling the French influence in Scotland, Margaret began to petition Parliament for an end to James's minority in the summer of 1523, but was knocked back. Parliament and the council expected Albany to return at any time and were loath to make any big decisions about the young king's future in his absence. After begging her brother for help, Margaret decided it would be better to take matters into her own hands and kidnap her son (who was just as keen to be liberated from the irksome close confinement that he was forced to endure) while he was out hunting at Stirling Castle. Her correspondent, Surrey, offered to help by sending his men over the border to attack Jedburgh, which he hoped would distract the Scots long enough for Margaret to seize her son, take him to Edinburgh and have him declared king in his own right, backed up by the money and men that her brother had promised to send her once her son's minority and the French alliance was at an end. Margaret was not fond of Surrey's daring plan, which targeted the very inhabitants of the borders that she had been trying her best to protect from English harassment – but also realised she had little choice but to comply. Her hesitancy would prove fatal however; before she could act, Albany landed at Leith that autumn with a small French fleet of twelve fully victualled ships bearing money, weapons, twenty-eight cannons, horses and 4,000 troops. Apprehensive about the duke's reaction when he discovered her plot to liberate her son, Margaret begged Surrey for help escaping to England; although he seemed keen to help, in reality he was loath to bring her into England and believed it would be better for everyone if she was left in Scotland.

Desperate to prove herself a loyal English subject, Margaret began to furnish Surrey with detailed descriptions of the French troops and armaments that Albany had brought back with him and also his plans for his campaign against the English – all of which were duly passed on to her brother and Wolsey. Albany had known for a long time that Margaret could not be trusted and was almost certainly aware of what she was up to, but Wolsey nonetheless feared for her safety, noting that if just one of her treacherous letters was intercepted by the duke, it might well lead to her 'final destruction'. Preoccupied with his plans for the English invasion, Albany resolved to deal with Margaret at a later date and in the meantime treated her and King James, who was living with her at Stirling Castle, with his usual unruffled politeness and courtesy. In truth, he had not really wanted to return to Scotland and was keen to return to France and his wife as soon as possible – but he had promised King François that he would support him by invading England, even if his heart was not entirely in it. By the end of October, he was on the other side of the border with his French troops and laying siege to the strategically important Wark Castle in Northumberland. However, he was forced to retreat after just three days, disheartened by the lack of support by his Scottish troops and unwilling to face Surrey in open battle.

When he returned to Edinburgh he took his frustrations out on Margaret, accusing her of colluding with the English to have James kidnapped and whisked across the border to England; he ordered her to leave Stirling immediately. Convinced that this time her brother would step in to save the day, Margaret openly defied Albany and refused to leave her son's side, even when the council also demanded she retire to another residence. It was only when Margaret was on the point of giving in that Albany relented and allowed her to remain.

Margaret's willingness to share the details of Albany's campaign had done her no favours with her brother and Surrey; she found herself overlooked and sidelined when Albany, who was keen to return home to France as soon as possible but could not while Scotland was still at loggerheads with England, approached them to arrange a truce. Margaret was hurt and confounded to receive no replies to the letters she sent across the border, and reproached Surrey and her brother for forgetting her. Keen to maintain French control in Scotland even in his absence, Albany attempted to take advantage of Margaret's distress by offering her sanctuary in France, along with a handsome pension. It must have been a tempting offer, but Margaret was determined never to leave her son's side and so she turned him down –

but not before ensuring that her brother got to hear about it, so he would know that she had other options should he let her down again. Relieved to be going home at last, Albany left Scotland on 31 May 1524, never to return.

Margaret wasted no time after his departure before forming a new alliance with the Earl of Arran and worked harder than ever to promote the end of her son's minority, even writing to Henry on 19 June to ask for his support. However, just as she believed that success and freedom was within her grasp, she received word that her estranged husband had managed to escape his enforced exile in France and was in London – and meeting with her brother. As Margaret read Henry's letter, she must have laughed derisively at the description of 'Our dearest cousin, the Earl of Angus, whom we find to be your obedient, loving and faithful servant and husband', before becoming progressively more alarmed by the news that Archibald was 'intending and minding none other thing but first to reconcile himself unto your grace and favour; and secondly, to interpose his help, study, travail and authority, to the conducing of such good peace between us.'

Margaret knew only too well that Archibald had no interest in anything other than advancing his own position and enriching himself, preferably with her money, and wrote to tell Henry so, reminding him that 'as to my lord of Angus and me, where your grace desireth me to take him in my favour; as to that, he hath not shown, since his departing out of Scotland, that he desired my good will and favour, neither by writing nor word.' She warned her brother that Archibald was exploiting him to further his own ends, but to no avail. Although Henry responded with a promise not to send Archibald back to Scotland until she had managed to secure her son's emancipation, Margaret knew that it was only a matter of time before her husband returned to cause trouble again.

On 26 July 1524, King James escaped from Stirling Castle, where he had been guarded by French soldiers left behind by Albany, and rode for Edinburgh, which he and his mother triumphantly entered together, greeted by ecstatic crowds who saw the liberation of the boy king as the beginning of a new, more peaceful and prosperous era for Scotland. After being invested as king with the crown, sceptre and sword of state, James took up residence in the royal apartments of Holyrood Palace and began to assert his authority as king in his own right – with his mother as the power behind the throne. He presided over his first council meeting less than a week later and formally requested that Albany's regency be brought to an end – a motion that was supported by almost all of his nobility, encouraged by Arran and the powerful Hamilton clan.

One of the few dissenting voices was that of James Beaton, Lord Chancellor of Scotland, longtime bête noir of Queen Margaret and loyal champion of the Scottish-French alliance. Incensed by his defiance, Margaret had him imprisoned along with anyone else who opposed her will. Almost eleven years had passed since the horror and disappointment of Flodden and in that time, Margaret had known barely a moment of peace as she fought opposition from all sides, schemed, wept and endured a seemingly endless parade of defeats and losses. Although hardly quick-witted or especially skilled in diplomacy, she had nonetheless done her best for her son despite the odds stacked against her and she must have felt relieved and happy as she watched him take his place as king at last. It added to her pleasure that for once she finally had the approval of her brother Henry, who wrote to congratulate her on her success and sent Dr Thomas Magnus, Archdeacon of the East Riding of Yorkshire as an emissary to her son's court, bearing valuable gifts, which included cloth-of-gold, money, a beautiful new sword and the Order of the Garter for the boy king. He also brought authorisation to renew negotiations for a betrothal between James and his cousin, Princess Mary of England. The only remaining issue was the ever constant spectre of her husband Archibald – he persisted in writing to her even though she returned his letters unopened and was still loudly protesting his innocence and devotion to his wife to anyone who would listen. Henry had allowed him to leave London but promised Margaret that he would not be allowed to travel past the border unless she gave him permission to do so, which of course, she was highly reluctant to give – not least because she had recently taken a lover and was keen to keep the fact a secret.

The new man in Margaret's life was the 29-year-old Henry Stewart, younger brother of Lord Ochiltree and son of Andrew Stewart, Lord Avondale, a distant cousin of Margaret's first husband James IV, who had perished alongside him and so many others at Flodden. As the second son of a relatively obscure nobleman, Stewart was not an especially important member of the Scottish royal court and had held the minor post of carver to the young king until he caught Margaret's eye and began to rise up through the ranks, eventually becoming her Captain of the Guard. Although the atmosphere at the Scottish court was as louche as ever and everyone remembered how promiscuous her first husband had been, Margaret was forced to be discreet while she continued to ask Albany to use his influence in the Vatican to procure her much longed for divorce from Archibald. She also knew that whatever small sympathy she received for her mistreatment at her husband's hands would vanish completely if it was known that she too was unfaithful. Men were, to an extent, expected to cheat on their wives but, however poorly they were treated by their husband, an unfaithful woman could expect no pity at all – as Margaret would have known all too well. Certainly she would have had every reason to fear another deluge of censorious letters from her brother and sister-in-law, Queen Catherine – with the latter feeling particularly strongly about the subject now that her influence over her husband had waned and he was becoming increasingly interested in the ladies of her household.

Although she had achieved the emancipation of her son, Margaret was still afraid that Albany might return to undo all her hard work, despite the fact that he had made it perfectly plain that he had absolutely no desire to ever set foot in Scotland ever again. As always, she turned to Henry for support, encouraged by the kindness he was currently lavishing upon her and her son, including a personal bodyguard of 200 well-trained men and large sums of money.

Henry, however, was a deeply misogynistic product of his era and although he demanded absolute loyalty from his sister, he had no real faith in either her abilities or her integrity. To his mind, her husband Archibald, whom he personally liked and believed would be faithful to English interests so long as English gold kept flowing in his direction, was the best hope for maintaining the status quo between their two kingdoms. Although Henry privately conceded that Margaret had every reason to free herself from Archibald, he could not approve of her attempts to secure a divorce and so continued to press her to reconcile with her husband, much to her annoyance. He was supported by Dacre and Wolsey, who continued to intercept the flow of letters between Scotland and England and meddle in Margaret's affairs, believing it would benefit everyone if she would stop complaining and take her husband back. By the start of October 1524, Archibald was being held in Newcastle with his brother George and itching to return home to Scotland. The feckless pair swore an oath to Surrey, who had recently succeeded his father as Duke of Norfolk, that they would do nothing to harm King James and would do everything in their power to further English interests and oppose those of France. Furthermore, Archibald faithfully promised to do everything in his power to 'recover the Queen's favour' and would not return to court until he had done so. The following day they were on their way back to Scotland and by the start of November, they had crossed the border and were beginning to amass men to their cause.

Margaret rightly blamed her brother, Wolsey, Dacre and Norfolk for Archibald's return and took her anger out on the unfortunate Magnus, who did his best to exonerate King Henry of blame but was completely unable to placate her and indeed would report to his masters that he felt it entirely unbecoming for someone of his poor rank to dare to remonstrate with a queen – especially a Tudor one throwing a right royal tantrum. It was widely expected that Archibald and the Douglases would gatecrash King James's first session of Parliament, which was to be held on 14 November, but to Margaret's relief the day passed without incident and was indeed a marked success; Albany's regency was formally ended and her own was approved without contest.

Archibald remained a threat though and eventually made his move in the early hours of 23 November when he sent men to scale the walls of Edinburgh and then open the gates to him, claiming that he had no wish to cause harm but had been forced to such measures by the perfidy of his wife, who was returning his letters unopened. Infuriated, Margaret immediately ordered that the castle guns be aimed at him, then once again lost her temper with Magnus when he remonstrated with her and, rather ill-advisedly, told her it was completely unseemly for a woman to fire upon her own husband, especially when he came in peace as Archibald had done.

After ordering him to go back to England and stop meddling in affairs that did not concern him, Margaret ordered that the guns were fired – missing Archibald, who decided that this was the moment to retreat back home to Tantallon Castle, but instead killing four innocent Edinburgh citizens. This action would make her the talk of Europe – much to her brother's great displeasure. Not that Margaret cared very much about that, for she immediately fired off a letter to Henry, accusing him of putting her son's life in danger by allowing Archibald to return to Scotland.

The stalemate between the warring couple continued well into the following year, with a lot of negotiating, meetings, threats and bargaining on both sides before Margaret, who feared his growing popularity and had belatedly come to realise her own meagre influence was beginning to disappear, grudgingly allowed Archibald and his men to return to Edinburgh. He visited their daughter, who was now 9-years-old and had barely seen her father. He was also allowed to participate in the state opening of the Scottish Parliament on 23 February and meekly bore the crown in the procession, which was headed by Margaret and her son King James, while his former rival Arran bore the sceptre and Argyll carried the sword of state.

Believing that Archibald was effectively neutralised, if only temporarily, Margaret was able to enjoy being in charge for once and at the beginning of 1525 she was corresponding in the most friendly terms with King François of France, who was very keen to continue the Auld Alliance with Scotland and offered Margaret enticements to do so, as well as sending her 5,000 gold crowns. After François's defeat and capture at the Battle of Pavia on 24 February 1525, the negotiations were taken over by his formidable mother Louise de Savoie, who offered Margaret a pension and home in France as well as the betrothal of King James to one of her granddaughters, the little Princesses of France. Henry was still dangling a betrothal with his daughter Mary, his only legitimate child and heiress at the time, but Louise reminded Margaret that her brother had already promised Mary to her cousin Emperor Charles, which would be a far more prestigious and useful match. Nonetheless, however tempted she might have been by the offer, Margaret ostentatiously turned it down, preferring to publicly place her trust in her brother and do what she could to encourage the match between James and Mary. She continued to exchange letters with Louise though and her secret correspondence with Albany continued as before. She charged him to let it be discreetly known in France that if her brother continued to support her husband against her, then she would join forces with the French against him. The duke was still trying his best to get her the divorce she longed for and in February 1525 she reminded him that she could be a more useful ally to the French if Archibald, who was in the pocket of her brother and a fully paid-up creature of the English, was no longer her husband.

While Margaret was scheming to get rid of Archibald, even if it meant making an enemy of her own brother, her estranged husband was busy writing letters to Henry and Wolsey, telling them that young James was being poorly looked-after by his mother, who was allowing herself to be led by 'evilly disposed persons' – namely her lover, Henry Stewart. In March, he wrote again to inform Wolsey that despite attempts to mediate between them, it was clear that Margaret was determined never to reconcile with him and so he wished to resume appropriating her rents – which by law belonged to him as her husband – and to have reassurance of Henry's support against her.

He was supported by the English ambassador, Magnus, who reported to Henry that although Margaret behaved tolerably well towards Archibald in public, in private she was trying to bribe him with money to agree to the divorce, motivated by her passion for Henry Stewart. He also reported that Margaret only behaved well if she wanted money but was otherwise almost impossible to deal with thanks to her mood swings and temper tantrums when thwarted. This situation was exacerbated when Henry took it upon himself to write her a letter of reproof, taking her to task for her 'unwifely' behaviour towards her husband and, worse still, her adultery with Henry Stewart. Magnus could only watch in horror as Margaret broke down in tears, deeply wounded by her brother's censure. Feeling attacked on all sides, she retreated to Stirling Castle with her lover and refused to appear at the next session of Parliament; this was a tactical error, for they seized the opportunity to remove her son from her care and instead place him under the guardianship of four noblemen, who would rotate their posts four times a year to ensure that the power was equally shared between them. To the surprise of absolutely no one, Archibald was to be one of his stepson's guardians, along with his fellow Earls of Arran, Lennox and Argyll, and to Margaret's dismay it was decided that he would be the first to take charge of the young king. It can't have been much of a surprise, especially to his wife, that when his period of guardianship came to an end on 1 November, Archibald simply refused to hand the king over to the next in line. Once again, he had won and it seemed like there was very little that Margaret, whose support had dwindled since his return to Scotland, could do about it.

Appalled by this effective kidnapping of her son, Margaret wasted no time before pulling together whatever support and manpower she could muster. The Douglas family were still deeply unpopular in Scotland and no matter what people thought of her personally, the other powerful Scottish lords were loath to see the Douglases wielding absolute power. The young king had never been overly fond of his stepfather, but absolutely loathed him now and secretly wrote to his mother to beg her to rescue him; at the same time, Archibald was forcing James to publicly declare that he was happy to remain under the care of the Douglas family, who were now placed in every possible high office. Archibald was not at all above using the boy to achieve his own ends, on at least one occasion making him ride closely beside him when they encountered Margaret's troops near Linlithgow – a ploy that ensured that she would never engage him in battle lest her precious son suffered. However, if Archibald had expected the other lords to bow their knees to him, he was proved wrong and quickly found himself losing support as a result of his coup. Yes, he had the king in his control, but he was becoming increasingly embattled as he struggled to keep hold of his prize.

Meanwhile, sympathy and support for Margaret was increasing all the time. Now that Arran had thrown his lot in with his former enemy Archibald, her chief supporter was the 36-year-old John Stewart, 3rd Earl of Lennox, a great grandson of James II, who was also in the line of succession for the Scottish throne. Having signed a bond with the young king in which he agreed to liberate him from the Douglases in exchange for being made

Lord Chancellor, Lennox and his 10,000 men took on Arran's significantly smaller troop of 2,500 at Linlithgow Bridge on 4 September 1526. It should have been an easy victory for Lennox but he was efficiently outmanoeuvred, defeated and then killed right before the horrified James.

Having destroyed Lennox, Archibald now turned his attention to Margaret, who was under siege in Stirling Castle with her lover Henry Stewart, eventually forcing her to abandon the castle and take flight. Despite this, the couple were able to put on a show of unity at the next meeting of the Scottish Parliament in November, which Margaret attended simply because it meant she would have an opportunity to see her son, who had been kept from her for several months. Exhausted and defeated, she agreed to keep the peace and make no more trouble for Archibald in exchange for being able to remain at court with her son. She had serious doubts about her husband's competence to act as a guardian for the boy and was willing to make any compromise in order to keep an eye on things – even if she was relatively powerless to intervene.

James V had turned 14 and officially attained his majority in April 1526, but despite his mother's best efforts to increase his independence, it made very little difference to his situation because his stepfather was determined not to relax his hold on power. He was doubtless also aware that the boy hated him, which would have made him extra keen not to let him seize power for himself. Intelligent, courageous and resourceful, James was desperate to rule in his own right but found himself effectively sidelined by the Douglases, who cynically attempted to distract him from his kingly duties and politics by instead interesting him in the usual court pursuits of hunting, gambling, drinking and women – all of which James enjoyed to excess – much to his mother's despair, for she realised that Archibald was trying to dissipate the young king in order to further his own interests.

As for Margaret, she did her best to remain in favour so that she could stay at court. At the start of 1527 she even found the time to turn her attention to the more pleasant occupation of arranging her young daughter's betrothal to a Scottish nobleman, before changing her mind and instead betrothing 11-year-old Margaret, who looked set to rival her famously lovely aunt Mary for beauty, to the young Earl of Lennox, son of her former ally. Attempts to arrange her own future happiness were less successful though and she fell out with her son in the spring when, encouraged by Archibald, he refused to allow Henry Stewart to join her household at court, causing Margaret to flounce back to Stirling, where she could live openly with her lover on her own terms. She would have been happier about the situation had she known that the divorce she had been longing for – to the point that she had even tried to claim there were plausible grounds to believe that her first husband had survived Flodden – had been granted by Pope Clement VII on 11 March, citing her husband's adultery. Thanks to the disruption that the wars had caused across Europe, Margaret did not find out that she was free of Archibald until December.

Archibald was predictably furious when he heard the news – although the couple had been estranged for the vast majority of their marriage, he derived much of his power and influence from being married to her and now this was at an end. Instead, the position of brother-in-law to Henry of England and stepfather of King James was to be taken by the relatively obscure Henry Stewart, whom Margaret married on 3 March 1528. Archibald forced Margaret to hand over their daughter and then made James ride with him to lay siege to Stirling Castle where Margaret and Henry were living together. While she was under violent attack from her former husband, Margaret was also forced to endure a bombardment of angry letters from England, all encouraging her to reconcile with Archibald for the sake of her immortal soul and the legitimacy of her daughter – ignoring the fact that Margaret Douglas's legitimacy had been confirmed by the Pope at the same time as he had approved her parents' divorce.

Wolsey and Catherine of Aragon both had plenty to say about the matter but most vicious of all was Margaret's brother Henry, who demanded that 'for the weal of your soul, and to avoid the inevitable damnation threatened against adulterers, to reconcile yourself with Angus as your true husband', before reminding her that:

> what danger of damnation should it be to your soul, with perpetual infamy of your renown, slanderously to distain with dishonour so goodly a creature, so virtuous a lady, and namely your natural child, procreate in lawful matrimony ... unless your Grace will (as in conscience ye are bound under peril of God's everlasting indignation) relinquish the adulterers company with him that is not, nor may be of right your husband.

In the past Margaret had been devastated by Henry's reproving letters, but the knowledge that he was currently pursuing a divorce so that he could marry Norfolk's niece Anne Boleyn meant she no longer felt intimidated by him and his hypocrisy.

It wasn't just Margaret who felt less intimidated by their male relatives – her 16-year-old son James had decided he'd had enough of Archibald and the Douglas family and was quietly hatching plans to escape their clutches. Although his stepfather had claimed that the young king was unhappy about his mother's remarriage, he was actually pleased enough to welcome Henry Stewart to the family, no doubt recognising that his mother had suffered enough tragedy and misfortune in her life and deserved a little happiness. He struck a deal with Margaret whereby he would give her marriage his blessing and bestow the title of Lord Methven upon her new husband in exchange for Stirling Castle. He then bided his time until an opportunity to escape presented itself during a hunting trip to Falkland Palace in the spring of 1528.

The young king, who had inherited all of his father's courage and a hefty dash of his mother's Tudor wilfulness, slipped away during the night along with a small group of trusted companions and rode to Stirling Castle, where he was welcomed by his mother and the Earl of Arran, and banned Archibald and the entire Douglas family from coming within seven miles of his person. The flight of the king marked the beginning of the end for the detested Earl of Angus. Although he still held Edinburgh, without the person of the king Archibald had little authority and could not prevent James and Margaret from seizing power and eventually ousting him from the capital, forcing him to retreat once again to his stronghold Tantallon Castle. In September, Archibald and his supporters were declared traitors and had their lands and goods seized before, encouraged by his mother, James laid siege to Tantallon, hoping to flush Archibald out so that he could have him executed. The siege did not go well and James was forced to withdraw, but hostilities continued to escalate until, in May 1529, Archibald, accompanied by his daughter Lady Margaret, slipped across the border into England, where he had been promised asylum by his erstwhile brother-in-law in exchange for taking an oath of allegiance and surrendering his lands to the Scottish crown. He did not return to Scotland until James's death in 1542.

Chapter 16

The Final Chapter 1529–1541

Margaret and Archibald were married for almost thirteen years and other than perhaps a few months at the beginning, had been at loggerheads for the entirety of their relationship. Their marriage had produced their daughter Margaret, but even she had been used as a weapon by her warring parents, neither of whom had taken much interest in her until she had become old enough to be used as an asset. After Archibald took young Margaret across the border to England, her mother made some half-hearted attempts to have her returned but was content when she learned that she had been taken to London and was being raised alongside her cousin Princess Mary. Although Margaret must have had some mixed feelings about her daughter being brought up in England, her fond memories of her own childhood in the luxurious surroundings of the Tudor royal palaces would have reassured her that it was in her daughter's best interests to grow up far away from the chaos and turmoil that was apt to manifest at any moment in Scotland. For James's part, he had never warmed to his younger half-sister and would insist upon referring to her as 'base born', even though her legitimacy had been confirmed by the Pope himself. Sadly for Lady Margaret, her brother's hatred of the entire Douglas clan would also extend to her and they would never enjoy a good relationship.

At long last, Margaret had the power, respect and influence that she had been fighting for ever since the death of James IV. Although her son was keen to rule for himself, he was also more than happy to be guided by Margaret and her husband, Lord Methven. It was precisely the sort of scenario that she had envisaged when she married Archibald Douglas and Margaret relished the opportunity to act as the power behind the throne, just as she had always wanted. She turned 40 in November 1529 and doubtless looked forward to several more decades living in comfort at her son's court or on her own estates with her husband at her side. It has been suggested that at some point in the first years of their marriage, the couple had a daughter, Dorothea Stewart, who died in infancy but her existence is by no means certain as there is no mention of her in the official records.

Certainly, for a while at least, Margaret's third marriage was much happier than her last one and she began the new decade feeling infinitely more confident and optimistic about the future than she had felt for a very long time. She and her son were closer than ever and she frequently joined him on his progresses around Scotland, including a visit in September 1532 to Blair Castle, the seat of John Stewart, 3rd Earl of Atholl, who spent a huge sum building a temporary green timber palace to house his royal guests, complete with moat, tapestry covered walls and glass windows. They spent three days there, enjoying excellent hunting during the day and lavish banquets in the evening, all of which cost their generous host a tremendous £1,000 a day. As they rode away, the earl ordered that the palace be set on fire as was the local custom, much to the astonishment of the Papal envoy, Sylvester Darius who had accompanied Margaret and James on their trip.

Thanks to her divorce and the departure of Archibald, Margaret was also feeling much wealthier than she had been for years. During his last unlawful period of supremacy over her son, Archibald had reasserted his right to misappropriate her lands, backed by the large cohorts of Douglas family members and supporters that he had planted in the royal household, council and Scottish Parliament, and had ended up seizing Doune Castle, Methven Castle, Newark Castle and Linlithgow Palace for himself, significantly reducing Margaret's income even more. Now though, much of her lands and revenue was restored, although her son retained Stirling Castle and Linlithgow Palace for himself. After over a decade of worrying about money and not being able to live in a style fitting for a dowager Queen of Scotland, Margaret was finally able to enjoy the trappings considered fitting for her station and did her son credit by always appearing magnificently dressed and bedecked in costly jewels, even spending the vast sum of £20,000 on clothes for a meeting between her brother and son that was fated never to take place.

Until James married, she continued to act as Queen of Scotland, presiding over court functions, meeting with foreign dignitaries and adding a touch of feminine glamour to state events. Her son had enjoyed a parade of mostly relatively high-born mistresses since his mid-teens, encouraged by Archibald, but these ladies are shadowy figures who seem to have discreetly remained on the outskirts of the court rather than enjoying the prominence that royal mistresses enjoyed at the French court. Like his father, he was also producing a significant brood of illegitimate children, at least three of whom had been fathered before he had reached the age of 20 and who were raised at court and treated with great favour by their father. As a young wife, Margaret had felt threatened by her husband's illegitimate children and jealous of their mothers – one wonders what she made of her son's amorous escapades and if she greeted this ever increasing brood of grandchildren with pleasure.

For the first half of the 1530s, Margaret was engrossed with promoting a good relationship between her son and brother King Henry, wilfully ignoring the fact that James had no desire to be friends with his uncle. It wasn't just the ever-present spectre of Flodden that hung over them, but also the fact that Henry was sheltering Archibald and providing him with a generous pension as well as continuing to meddle in Scottish affairs. No doubt James was also well aware of his uncle's claims that Scotland was merely a vassal state of England and that the Kings of Scotland owed him their fealty. Margaret would expend a lot of energy trying to arrange a meeting between the two, only to be defeated by James's apathy and unwillingness to cross the border into England. The matter was complicated by Henry's divorce from Catherine of Aragon, which had resulted in a schism between England and the Catholic church of Rome and, by extension, a division between Henry and the other crowned heads of Europe, which would affect his relationship with them for the rest of his reign.

As a devout Catholic, James was naturally appalled by his uncle's apparently reckless behaviour and it hardened his resolve not to meet with him and put their distant relationship on more familiar terms. Nonetheless, in 1533 Margaret and Henry exchanged a flurry of letters, their first for quite some time, discussing the possibility of a meeting between the two kings, with Margaret pretending that her son was as eager for the meeting as she was, even claiming that James had 'affectionately desired us to write in his name unto you ... that not only will he meet, and commune, and visit you, but also loves your Grace better than any man living next himself.' Now that her life was more peaceful, Margaret had been thinking a great deal about visiting England and she was no doubt keen to see her daughter, who turned 18 in October 1533 and was one of the brightest stars of her uncle's court. Sadly there was no hope of a reunion with her sister Mary though, for the Duchess of Suffolk passed away in June 1533, leaving Margaret and Henry as the last two surviving Tudor siblings – not that this improved the relationship between them, despite Margaret's best efforts. 'Your Grace is our only brother, and we your only sister,' she reminded him in December 1533, 'and since so is, let no divorce or contrary have place, nor no report of ill-advised persons alter our conceits, both brotherly and sisterly love ever to endure, to the pleasure of God and weal of us both; and trust no less in me than in yourself.'

At the start of 1536, James finally gave in to his mother's demands and agreed to meet with his uncle, but their plans quickly stalled when Henry suggested that the meeting take place at York and James countered by insisting that he would go no further into England than Newcastle. The dramatic fall from grace and execution of Henry's second wife Anne Boleyn in May 1536 also effectively put paid to their plans; Henry was in no mood to see his nephew, who was, in the eyes of many at least, heir presumptive to the English throne now that both of Henry's daughters, Mary and Elizabeth, had been declared illegitimate and removed from the succession. There was some talk that James should marry the elder girl, Mary, who was four years his junior, but James rejected the match on the grounds that it would not be fitting for an anointed king to marry a woman who had been declared illegitimate by her own father.

It would soon transpire, much to his mother's despair, that James had made matrimonial plans of his own and was keen to marry his latest and most favourite mistress Margaret Erskine, who was rather inconveniently already married to Sir Robert Douglas of Lochleven. Margaret Erskine had already given birth to the king's favourite son, James, who would be made Earl of Moray and, perhaps encouraged by his uncle's successful campaign to marry Anne Boleyn for love, James now obtained a Scottish divorce for his mistress before turning his attention to the Pope, who would be able to end Margaret's marriage while at the same time ensuring the legitimacy of any future children they might have. His mother was appalled – she had fought long and hard for her son's right to rule, only to have him throw away his dignity with what she saw as a tawdry match which would put him at loggerheads with half of his nobility. Thanks to bitter experience, she had finally come to realise just how deep the rivalries and loyalties of the numerous Scottish clans ran and she had experienced for herself just how polarising such a match would be as it gave power to the family and friends of the new royal bride and infuriated and alienated the enemies of her clan, not to mention the family of her now estranged husband.

To Margaret's enormous relief, Pope Paul III refused to approve Margaret Erskine's divorce and her son, whom she no doubt feared would react as his uncle had done to being similarly thwarted in his Great Matter, accepted the Papal decision meekly and instead turned his attention to making a more prestigious match with France. During his regency and even afterwards, Albany had never ceased to promote a match between James and one of

King François's four daughters but by 1536, only two remained alive – 16-year-old Madeleine, who was extremely frail, and 13-year-old Marguerite. Unwilling to sacrifice either of his adored daughters to the famously cold Scottish climate, François had dissuaded James from seeking the hand of either of them and instead offered Marie de Bourbon, daughter of the Duc de Vendôme. James was less than keen to marry a mere noblewoman rather than a princess of the blood, but he was determined to forge closer ties to the French, not least because it would annoy his uncle Henry, and so he duly set off for France on 23 July 1536.

To her delight, Margaret was left to act as regent in his absence, maybe even for several months – and indeed James would not return to Scotland until May 1537. After her failed attempt to arrange a meeting between James and her brother, Margaret had become depressed as she realised that her son no longer required her advice or support and was not prepared to let her rule through him any more. Dejected, she complained about feeling 'weary of Scotland', but there was no place for her in England either. Her brother's chief minister Thomas Cromwell, who had replaced Wolsey after his fall from grace, made it clear that she was not welcome to visit when she offered to come instead of her son, and when she asked her brother to recompense her for the money she had wasted on preparations for his cancelled meeting with her son, he gave her equally short shrift. However, relations between Henry and Margaret would plummet to an all time low in August when an English messenger arrived in Perth, where Margaret was residing, with the alarming news that her daughter had been arrested and was in serious danger of being executed.

Lady Margaret Douglas was 20-years-old, very pretty, headstrong, lively, flirtatious and intelligent. She was extremely popular at the English court and enjoyed significant favour from her uncle, who showered her with gifts and even hinted that he was considering making her his heir now that both of his daughters had been disinherited. Everyone expected Lady Margaret to one day make an advantageous match, perhaps even to a foreign prince, which made it all the more shocking when it was revealed that she had secretly become engaged to Lord Thomas Howard, a younger half-brother of the Duke of Norfolk and uncle to the disgraced and executed Anne Boleyn. Youthful flirtations and clandestine relationships were a normal part of court life, but as Margaret was so dangerously close to the throne and required her uncle's permission to marry, the pair found themselves summarily arrested and imprisoned in the Tower of London, which must have been a terrifying experience – especially as only a few months had passed since the swift fall from grace of Anne Boleyn and her alleged lovers. That Lord Thomas was a member of the Howard family, who were now very much out of favour at court thanks to Queen Anne's downfall, only added to Henry's fury and while he might at another time have excused the incident as a mere youthful indiscretion, he now chose to regard it in a far more sinister light and accused the pair of having designs upon his throne, aided and abetted by Lady Margaret's mother, his sister Margaret.

When the news arrived of her daughter's imprisonment, Margaret fell into a panic and immediately fired off a letter to her brother in which she denied all knowledge of the affair and begged him to treat the unfortunate girl with leniency, reminding him that Lady Margaret was his own niece, the daughter of his only surviving sister:

> Dearest brother, we beseech your Grace, of sisterly kindness and natural love we bear, and that you owe to us your only sister, to have compassion and pity of us your sister, and of our natural daughter and sister to the king our only natural son and your dearest nephew; and to grant to our said daughter Margaret your Grace's pardon, grace and favour, and remit of such as your Grace has put to her charge.

She even went on to request that Lady Margaret should be sent back to her in Scotland – no doubt knowing that Henry would never agree to it, having been at some pains ever since her arrival in England to ensure that his niece should not be kidnapped and taken back to her mother.

Margaret closed her heartfelt missive with the words:

> And this, dearest brother, we, in our most hearty, affectionate, tender manner, most specially and most humbly beseech your Grace to do, as we doubt not your wisdom will think to your honour, since this our request is dear and tender to us, the gentlewoman's natural mother, and we your natural sister, that makes this piteous and most humble request.

Shortly after her letter arrived in London, Lady Margaret had been pardoned and transferred from the Tower of London, where she had fallen ill, to the far more salubrious environs of Syon Abbey, where she was placed in the care of the nuns until her uncle felt able to welcome her back to court and his favour. Her lover Lord Thomas was far less fortunate and would remain incarcerated in the Tower until he died of an illness in October 1537, just a few days after Lady Margaret was released from captivity and allowed to return to court. Deeply relieved, Margaret wrote to thank her brother for pardoning her daughter, assuring him that she was just as horrified as him and that Lady Margaret 'will never have my blessing if she do not do all you command her'. Henry's response was to assure his sister that although her daughter had disgraced herself and 'used herself so lightly as was greatly to our dishonour and her own great hindrance', he would 'be good to her' in future and bear no grudge.

Having witnessed the callous way that Henry treated those who displeased him, even his own wives and children, Margaret had every reason to fear for her daughter as she navigated the dangerous world of the Tudor court, but she also accepted that there was very little that she could do to help other than to remain watchful and council Lady Margaret to tread carefully from now on – advice that evidently fell on deaf ears for she would be back in her uncle's bad books again within four years after having another clandestine affair with yet another member of the Howard family, this time with Queen Catherine Howard's brother Lord Charles Howard, a half-nephew of her first lover Lord Thomas – it seems that like her uncle, Lady Margaret Douglas had something of a fatal weakness for the Howards.

Relieved that her daughter had come to no great harm, Margaret was able to enjoy a few months of relative calm before she found herself plunged into yet another domestic drama at the beginning of 1537 – this time provoked by the unwelcome revelation that her second husband Lord Methven had been unfaithful to her with Lady Janet Stewart, a sister of the 3rd Duke of Atholl, who had entertained Margaret and her son James so lavishly at Blair Castle in 1532. To Margaret's distress and disappointment, she learned that just like Archibald, Methven had been diverting her money into his own coffers and had housed Lady Janet and their son in one of Margaret's own castles. It was a terrible blow and once again Margaret found herself contemplating divorce. Her brother was not especially sympathetic to her plight but no doubt felt that his own chequered marital career made him less qualified than before to lecture Margaret to stick with her philandering husband no matter what.

Once again, Margaret complained about a lack of money, claiming that not only was Methven stealing from her, but also that her son had left her without any funds while he was away in France. In response, Henry sent Ralph Sadler, a favourite protege of Thomas Cromwell, up to Scotland to discover the truth of the situation and assuage his sister's most pressing needs with a gift of £200, after which he was sent off to France to discuss the situation with King James, who was preparing to return home with his new wife. After his meeting with Marie de Bourbon, James had rather rudely repudiated the proposed match with her and instead travelled on to the French court, where he pressed King François to let him marry Princess Madeleine as had been originally planned. Although François remained unwilling to let his eldest surviving daughter leave France, he was eventually cajoled into agreeing to the match, encouraged by the fact that the winsome Madeleine had taken one look at the handsome young Scottish king and declared that she would have no other husband but him.

The couple were married in Paris on New Year's Day 1537 and returned to Scotland in May, accompanied by ships piled high with gifts from Madeleine's doting father. They landed at Leith on 19 May, where Madeleine won hearts by immediately kneeling on the shore and kissing the sand to signal her great happiness at finally arriving in her new country. Their happiness was to be short lived though; within just a few weeks, weakened by her lengthy journey, Madeleine had fallen desperately ill and on 7 July, died in the queen's apartments of Holyrood Palace with James at her side. She was just 16-years-old.

James was deeply distressed by the loss of his young wife and in no mood to listen to his mother's complaints about her mistreatment at the hands of Methven. At another time, he would doubtless have behaved less harshly towards her but when rumours, put about by Methven and his supporters, that Margaret was planning to remarry Archibald reached his ears, he allowed his absolute loathing of the Douglas family – and fear that they might once again seize power – to overwhelm him and immediately went on the defensive.

Realising that her son needed some persuasion, Margaret offered him her castle and estates at Dunbar in exchange for his approval, but James took the lands while still withholding his consent to her divorce, instead counselling her to return to her husband even though she assured him that she had absolutely no intention of remarrying Archibald and had in fact resolved to become a nun. In despair, Margaret threatened to leave Scotland for good and fled for the border, only to be caught by her son's men and ignominiously returned to Stirling Castle, where she wrote to Thomas Cromwell that her son was 'more unkind to me daily, and I would rather be dead than treated as I am'. Her situation was a truly pitiful one, but as far as her male relatives and their advisors were concerned, it was one she had brought upon herself by making reckless decisions, especially when it came to matters of the heart. She had come to expect her brother's censure, but it really hurt to have lost the approval of her son as well – especially as, to her mind at least, she had suffered so much on his behalf. One thing was clear though, without James's help, there was no way that she would be able to rid herself of Lord Methven and so she was forced to make peace with her third husband. They would never again live together as husband and wife but at least all talk of divorce was dropped, much to the relief of her son and brother.

Although James continued to sincerely mourn Madeleine, he wasted very little time before requesting another French bride to cement his alliance with King François. Naturally he would have preferred Madeleine's younger sister Marguerite, but instead was offered the recently widowed Marie de Guise, Duchesse de Longueville, who was a cousin of the rejected Marie de Bourbon. Marie de Guise was very attractive, unusually tall, extremely healthy and of proven fertility, having presented her now deceased husband with two strapping sons – it was not really surprising therefore that James's recently widowed uncle Henry should also have expressed an interest in taking Marie as his fourth wife. Although her father, the Duc de Guise, was rather tempted by the prospect of seeing his daughter as Queen of England, Marie herself, who was no fool, was not in the slightest bit impressed by Henry's suit and scornfully remarked that although 'I am big in person, I only have a small neck'. Besides which, François had offered her to James first and was inclined to honour his agreement with Scotland even if it offended Henry of England. Marie was duly married to James by proxy in May 1538 before departing almost immediately for Scotland, leaving her surviving son behind in France.

Margaret barely had a chance to know her first daughter-in-law Madeleine de Valois before she died and must have wondered what her son's latest bride would be like – especially as she was not a malleable teenager, but instead a mature woman of 22 who clearly knew her own mind and had a reputation for being extremely intelligent and cultivated. Anxious to make a good impression, Margaret asked her brother for money to buy new dresses so that she would look her best when Marie arrived, no doubt aware that the new Queen of Scotland would arrive with an extensive wardrobe of sophisticated and extremely fashionable French gowns and accessories. Margaret had always felt a certain insecurity about her appearance and never more so than now, although she need not have worried about her relationship with her new daughter-in-law, for Marie, who was naturally warm and got on with almost everyone, treated her with great kindness and in fact encouraged her husband James to be nicer to his mother as well. 'I have been much in her company,' Margaret would write to her brother about Marie, 'and she bears herself very honourably to me, with very good entertaining.'

With an energetic and charming young French queen presiding over the court, Margaret could now step back from the spotlight and enjoy her retirement. Unsuited to politics and diplomacy she had nonetheless tried her best, but had struggled when dealing with more ruthless tacticians such as her second husband Archibald, Albany, Wolsey and her brother. She had experienced tragedies, losses and betrayals that would have broken a weaker woman but instead she had pressed on no matter how exhausted and dispirited she might have been. All she had ever wanted from life was to live in comfort and at last, at the age of nearly 50, she was to have her wish. Although she had her own lands, she was often at court and spent most of her time with her daughter-in-law Marie, who was extremely devout and encouraged Margaret to become more pious in her twilight years, leading the Duke of Norfolk to report back to Henry that 'the young Queen is all Papist, and the old Queen nearly as much so'. However, although she was consoled by the kind attentions of Marie de Guise, Margaret still sought her brother's approval and was just as hurt as ever when it was not forthcoming.

In February 1540, Ralph Sadler was once again in Scotland to meet with James and asked for permission to see Margaret, which was gladly given with the young king telling Sadler: 'Ye need not ask my licence for that, but ye may boldly see and visit her at all times.' Although Sadler informed Margaret that he had come at her brother's behest and that Henry had asked him to see how she was doing, Margaret was not in the slightest bit appeased and as Sadler put it:

> She took it the most unkindly that might be, that she had no letter from your Highness, saying that she perceived that your Grace set not much store by her. But, quoth she, though I be forgot in England, shall I never forget England. It had been but a small matter ... to have spent a little paper and ink upon me and much it had been to my comfort; and were it perceived that the King's Grace my brother did regard me, I should be the better regarded of all parties here.

To reinforce just how poorly she believed herself to have been treated by her own brother, Margaret then talked at length about how well she got on with her daughter-in-law Marie de Guise, who paid her every possible attention and treated her with the greatest respect and affection. Their relationship became even closer when Marie, who was pregnant at the time of Sadler's visit, gave birth to a son James, Duke of Rothesay on 22 May 1540.

Although her husband had numerous other illegitimate children by this point, Prince James was his first legitimate son and his birth was greeted with great celebration and excitement, not least by Margaret who was delighted and relieved to see the Scottish royal line secured for the future.

James was followed a year later by a brother, Robert, who was born on 12 April 1541 and given the title of Duke of Albany – the regent who had been such a thorn in Margaret's side having died in June 1536. Sadly though, the Scottish royal family's joy at the birth of Prince Robert was to be short lived for the baby died on 20 April, followed less than twenty-four hours later by his older brother. James and Marie were devastated by the cruel loss of their children and Margaret was on hand to comfort them both, spending hours with both grieving parents and doing all that she could to lighten their burden. On 12 May, Margaret wrote to her brother from Stirling Castle that:

> here hath been great displeasure for the death of the prince and his brother, both with the king, my dearest son, and the Queen his wife; wherefore I have done great diligence to put them in comfort, and am never from them, but ever in their company, whereof they are very glad. Herefore I pray your Grace to hold me excused, that I write not at length of my matters at this time, because I can get no leisure.

Margaret's relationship with her brother was relatively cordial at this time and became increasingly so as once again plans were made for the two kings to meet while Henry was visiting York with his new wife Catherine Howard. Margaret had always regarded herself as a living symbol of the alliance between England and Scotland and took her role as peacemaker between the two very seriously, despite the best efforts of her brother, husbands, and now her son, to thwart her noble endeavours. It had been her dearest wish for quite some time that James and Henry should meet face to face and enjoy a close familial relationship, and now it looked as though all of her plans were to come to fruition. The fact that Margaret's daughter Lady Margaret Douglas, who was a lady-in-waiting of the new queen, would be present only made her more determined to bring the meeting about.

The much-anticipated meeting was set for September but at the very last minute James decided not to go, fearing that his uncle might have him kidnapped. Henry was incensed and so offended to be snubbed by his nephew that even Margaret who, despite everything, had always remained optimistic that a better understanding could be reached between their two nations, knew there was no way her brother would forgive such a slight and that another war was inevitable. Deeply depressed, she left court in October and took refuge at Methven Castle in Perthshire to recuperate. She suffered a stroke shortly after arriving but although she was forced to take to her bed to recover, she did not think her condition was sufficiently alarming to write a will or send for her son, who was staying at Falkland Palace. By the time James was informed of his mother's illness it was too late, and although he rode hard to be there at her side, he arrived at Methven Castle shortly after Margaret passed away on 18 October. She was 52-years-old.

'She took a palsy upon the Friday before night, at Methven, and died on the Tuesday following before night, but, as she doubted no danger of death, omitted to make her last will until past remembrance for that purpose,' the Berwick Pursuivant reported back to Henry's Privy Council later,

> She sent to Falkland for the king, her son, who came not till after she was departed. Seeing death approach, she desired the friars, her confessors, on their knees, to beseech the king to be gracious to the Earl of Angus, and asked God mercy that she had so offended the Earl.

She then made them promise to 'solicit from the King, her son, from her, to be good unto the Lady Margaret Douglas, her daughter, and that she might have of her goods, thinking it most convenient for her, forasmuch as she never had no thing of her before.' However, James had no desire to see any of his mother's belongings ending up in the hands of the Douglas family, so decided to give her jewels and other goods to his wife instead, while keeping the £2,500 in cash that she had left behind for himself. His sister would have nothing to console herself with, other than the fact that despite them having not set eyes on each other for several years, she had still been on her mother's mind as she lay on her deathbed.

Margaret Tudor, eldest daughter of Henry VII and Elizabeth of York, the first Tudor princess and Queen of Scotland, was buried with great pomp and ceremony in the Carthusian Charterhouse in Perth, which was also the final resting place of James I and his English queen Joan Beaufort. As Margaret had left no instructions for her burial, her son made all the arrangements, ensuring that his mother had the status and dignity in death that she had too often been denied in life.

* * *

Bibliography

Borman, Tracy, *The Private Lives of the Tudors*, Hodder (2017)

Borman, Tracy, *Thomas Cromwell*, Hodder and Stoughton (2014)

Clegg, Melanie, *Scourge of Henry VIII: The Life of Marie de Guise*, Pen & Sword (2016)

De Lisle, Leandra, *Tudor: The Family Story*, Vintage (2014)

Dunbar, John G, *Scottish Royal Palaces*, Historic Royal Scotland (1999)

Fraser, Antonia, *Mary Queen of Scots*, Weidenfeld and Nicolson (1969)

Fraser, Antonia, *The Wives of Henry VIII*, Vintage (1994)

Goodwin, George, *Fatal Rivalry, Flodden 1513*, W&N (2014)

Gristwood, Sarah, *Game of Queens*, Oneworld (2017)

Harrison, John G, *Ladies in Waiting: Marie de Guise at Stirling* (2008)

Harrison, John G, *Rebirth of a Palace: The Royal Court at Stirling Castle,* Historic Scotland (2011)

Kaufmann, Miranda, *Black Tudors: The Untold Story,* Oneworld (2017)

Macdougall, Norman, *James IV*, John Donald (2015)

Marshall, Rosalind K, *Mary of Guise: Queen of Scots*, Collins (1977)

Penn, Thomas, *Winter King: The Dawn of Tudor England*, Penguin (2011)

Perry, Maria, *Sisters of the King*, Andre Deutsch (1998)

Porter, Linda, *Crown of Thistles: The Fatal Inheritance of Mary Queen of Scots*, Pan (2013)

Scarisbrick, J.J., *Henry VIII*, Yale University Press (1997)

Starkey, David, *Henry: Virtuous Prince*, Harper (2009)

Thomas, Andrea, *Glory and Honour: The Renaissance in Scotland*, Birlinn (2013)

Thomas, Andrea, *Princelie Majestie: The Court of James V of Scotland*, John Donald (2005)

Tremlett, Giles, *Catherine of Aragon: Henry's Spanish Queen*, Faber & Faber (2011)

BIBLIOGRAPHY

Weir, Alison, *Elizabeth of York: The First Tudor Queen*, Vintage (2014)

Weir, Alison, *Henry VIII: King and Court*, Jonathan Cape (2001)

Weir, Alison, *The Lost Tudor Princess*, Vintage (2016)

Weir, Alison, *The Six Wives of Henry VIII*, Bodley Head (1991)

* * *

Index

INDEX

Beaufort, Lady Margaret, Countess
of Richmond and Derby, 5, 7, 9,
13-14, 21, 33-34, 44, 47-49, 54,
70, 74, 82, 91-92, 96, 133
Benolt, Thomas, 144, 145
Berkeley, Anne Fiennes,
Marchioness of, 6, 7
Bermondsey Abbey, 5
Berwick, 55-57, 88, 97, 106, 126,
138, 146
Biwimble, Alice, 7
Black Ellen, 85
Black Margaret, 85
Blackadder Castle, 126
Blair Castle, 161, 166
Boleyn, Anne, 35, 158, 163, 164, 165
Boleyn, Sir Thomas, 52
Bosworth, Battle of, 1, 2, 3, 30, 32,
38, 50, 53, 55
Bothwell, Patrick Hepburn, 1st Earl
of, 36, 37, 38, 53, 105, 113
Bourbon, Marie de, 164, 167, 168
Boyd, Marion, 21, 48, 75, 105, 138
Brandon, Charles (Duke of
Suffolk), 38, 114, 119, 120,
121, 133
Brandon, Henry, 134
Branxton, 105
Brinkburn Priory, 129
Brittany, Anne of (Queen of
France), 28, 103, 112
Bruce Castle, 133
Burgundy, Margaret of York,
Dowager Duchess of, 14, 16
Butler, Eleanor, 1, 7, 48

Calais, 32, 104, 142
Canterbury, Archbishop of
(John Morton), 6

Canterbury Cathedral, 6
Carlisle, 146
Cartington Castle, 129
Castile, Isabella of (Queen of
Spain), 7, 18, 20, 24, 27-31,
35-36, 39
Castile, Juana of, 32, 90, 91
Chadworth, Friar, 141
Charles V, Holy Roman Emperor,
32, 91, 114, 146, 155
Charles II of England, 19
Charles VIII of France, 2, 13
Chichester, Bishop of, 37
Clarence, George Plantagenet,
Duke of, 30
Cleves, Anne of (Queen of
England), 58
Cockburnspath, 36
Coldharbour, 16
Coldstream, 16, 126, 127, 147
Collyweston, 49, 50, 52
Compton, Sir William, 133
Comyn, Sir William, 104, 116,
117, 122
Craigmillar Castle, 139
Crichton, Sir Patrick, 139
Cromwell, Thomas, 164, 166, 167
Currour, John, 66

Dacre, Lady, 128, 131, 132
Dacre, Lord, 55, 81, 96, 98, 106,
109, 114, 117-118, 120, 122-132,
138-141, 143-146, 153
Dalkeith, 57, 59, 60, 61, 105
Damian, John, 75, 77, 86
Darius, Sylvester, 161
Darlington, 54
Darnaway Castle, 74
Davy, Alice, 7

175

INDEX

* * *